COLORS IN CAMBRIDGE GLASS II

IDENTIFICATION AND VALUE GUIDE

National Cambridge Collectors, Inc.

COLLECTOR BOOKS
A Division of Schroeder Publishing Co., Inc.

On the front cover:
Moonlight Caprice #165 6", three-footed candy box and cover. $100.00.
Peach-blo #1222 turkey. $800.00.
Crown Tuscan #1309, 5" vase, etched Portia, gold encrusted. $125.00.
Windsor Blue Seashell SS#40, 10" flower or fruit center. $3,000.00.

On the back cover:
Carmen Wild Rose #3200 punch bowl and base. $1,500.00.
Mardi Gras 1A, 12" vase. $1,000.00.
Crown Tuscan #1336, 18" vase, etched Rose Point, gold encrusted.*

*Due to the uniqueness of this item, no value is provided.

Cover design by Beth Summers
Book design by Barry Buchanan
Photography by Michael Neilson

COLLECTOR BOOKS
P.O. Box 3009
Paducah, Kentucky 42002-3009

www.collectorbooks.com

Copyright © 2007 National Cambridge Collectors, Inc.

The current values in this book should be used only as a guide. They are not intended to set prices, which vary from one section of the country to another. Auction prices as well as dealer prices vary greatly and are affected by condition as well as demand. Neither the authors nor the publisher assumes responsibility for any losses that might be incurred as a result of consulting this guide.

Searching for a Publisher?

We are always looking for people knowledgeable within their fields. If you feel that there is a real need for a book on your collectible subject and have a large comprehensive collection, contact Collector Books.

Proudly printed and bound in the
United States of America

CONTENTS

This book is dedicated to
the honor and memory of
all those who worked at the
Cambridge Glass Company
1902 – 1959.

The Cambridge Glass Co. was chartered in 1901 as an Ohio corporation and began producing glass in 1902. It was founded by the Pittsburgh-based National Glass Company as an independent company, not as a wholly owned subsidiary. National Glass Company engaged Arthur J. Bennett, an East Coast importer of glass and china, to manage the new Cambridge Glass Co. It began operations using molds from other National Glass companies and this ware is virtually impossible to distinguish from that produced by the original mold owners. It is not known if colored glass was produced during the first year of operation but by the time the 1903 catalog was issued, novelties as well as photographers' trays were being offered in colors such as opal, turquoise, green, amber, and blue. By 1906 Cambridge had begun to produce original designs, primarily in clear glass.

Arthur J. Bennett, by 1907, was the majority stockholder of the Cambridge Glass Co. and in 1910 the company acquired possession of the factory buildings, land, and equipment and thus became a truly independent company. Mr. Bennett remained the majority stockholder until 1939 when he sold controlling interest to his son-in-law, Wilbur Lofland Orme. Mr. Bennett continued as company president until his death in February 1940. At that time Mr. Orme assumed the presidency, a position he held until the summer of 1954 when the company was sold to Sidney Albert, an Akron, Ohio, industrialist, and operations ceased. In early 1955, after a series of legal maneuvers, a second Cambridge Glass Co. was formed and it assumed control of the original company's assets. In March 1955, the new company, staffed mainly with workers from the original company, began producing glass, mostly lines made by the first company. New lines and colors were introduced during the next three years but the second company was never as successful as the first. The second company continued to produce glass until late 1958 when manufacturing operations ceased. Sales of existing stock continued during 1959 and then in 1960 the remaining stock, molds, etching plates, and equipment were sold to Imperial Glass Corporation.

Color played an important role in making the Cambridge Glass Co. the success it was. As previously mentioned, color was in the original Cambridge catalog and, with perhaps only one or two exceptions, was in every general line catalog from then until the final price list was issued by the second company. Ebony, introduced in 1916, was the first important color for Cambridge and was quite popular at the time. While not a true color, Cambridge was second only to Fenton in introducing what we now know as carnival glass. During the early to middle 1920s Cambridge emphasized opaque colors and then gradually shifted to transparents; first light shades and then in the 1930s the darker colors such as Carmen, Forest Green, Amethyst, and Royal Blue. Throughout the 1930s, Cambridge continued to produce colored glass; but, by the end of that decade, new lines were mostly made in Crystal with Caprice being a notable exception. After the colors used with the Caprice line — Pistachio, Mocha, La Rosa, and Moonlight — were introduced between 1936 and 1938, no new colors were brought out until 1949. Numerous colors popular during the 1930s and early 1940s were discontinued in October 1943 due to wartime shortages and production of many never resumed. The second company's catalog and price lists offered colored glass but with the changing tastes of the buying public, it never achieved the popularity it once had.

Illustrated in this volume are 47 colors commercially produced by the original company and seven colors introduced by the second Cambridge Glass Co. Little is known about the chemists and other workers who formulated and initially produced most of these colors as few company records survive. Through verbal communications with a granddaughter, we do know that Arnold Fiedler, a German chemist, worked at Cambridge from about 1916 – 17 through the mid-1920s and was probably responsible for the colors introduced during that time period. Henry Hellmers, a well known glass chemist, worked at Cambridge during the early 1930s and among his contributions were Crown Tuscan, Carmen, Heatherbloom, Amethyst, and Forest Green.

With the earliest colors presented first, this book is arranged in chronological order based on the year each color was introduced. Thus, the reader can follow the evolution of the Cambridge lines through the years by reading each color in the order it is presented. Completing the book are plates showing color comparisons and several of the lines Cambridge was noted for: swans, the Statuesque line, figural flower frogs, and stemware.

Unless otherwise specified, when it is stated a piece is signed, the signature is the "C in a triangle."

This current volume would not have been possible without the contributions of Cynthia Arent, Carl Beynon, Sharon Miller, Judy Momirov, Mike and Lisa Neilson, Mark Nye, Mike Strebler, Lorraine Weinman, Lynn Welker, Frank Wollenhaupt, and all those who loaned glass to augment the museum collection. Not to be forgotten are the NCC, Inc. pioneers who, over 20 years ago, produced the original *Colors in Cambridge Glass*. Your efforts remain appreciated.

Cambridge began production early in May 1902. Its first known catalog was issued the following year. Novelty items in the colors of Opal, Turquoise, Blue, and Amber were offered as were photographers' supplies, such as trays and fixing boxes in Green and Amber. Three years later, in 1906, a price list offered the same colors with the exception of Opal and Turquoise which apparently had been discontinued.

Opal is a white that ranges from translucent to opaque. The white color varies from a good true white to various degrees of slight grayish or brownish tones.

Turquoise is a greenish blue opaque that trends more to the blue than to green.

There are no confirmed examples of the 1903 Blue. It is apparently a transparent blue of unknown density.

The 1903 Amber is a rather lifeless transparent color of medium density.

Green from 1903 is a deep transparent color that varies in density, from pure green to olive to emerald.

Identification of these early colors is complicated by the fact that none of the molds used during the first few years were original to Cambridge. Consequently, they could have been used by their original owners to produce colored glass similar to that produced by Cambridge.

By 1906 Cambridge was using some original molds and by 1910 producing original child sets. These are found in several shades of a transparent green which may or may not be the same as the 1903 green used to produce photographers' trays. The child's sets are also found in an early version of a dark blue, known as Early Cobalt and sometimes called early Royal Blue.

Row 1
1) Early Dark Emerald #2636, 9" nappy, E shape. $75.00.
2) Green # 671, 1 ounce cordial (called Blazing Cornucopia by collectors). $60.00.
3) Early Cobalt #2635 Fernland toy spooner. $30.00.
4) Early Cobalt #2631 Marjorie 5" nappy. $125.00.
5) Early Cobalt #2635 Fernland toy butter. $50.00.
6) Early Cobalt #2635 Fernland toy creamer. $30.00.
7) Early Cobalt #2635 Fernland toy sugar. $45.00.
8) Amber #1, 8¾" crucifix candlestick. $75.00.

Row 2
1) Opal "Queen" salt and pepper shakers with tray. $50.00 set.
2) Opal #1, 8¾" crucifix candlestick. $45.00.
3) Turquoise "Queen" salt and pepper shakers with tray. $100.00 set.
4) Turquoise "Saratoga" hat toothpick or match holder. $30.00.
5) Turquoise bird seed cup. $55.00.
6) Turquoise 7" trefoil plate. $40.00.

Plate 1

In January 1916, Cambridge introduced the first of the three colors it was to name Emerald. Trade journal reports of the day referred to it as emerald green or simply as green. This early Emerald is a dark transparent shade of green and is recognized by the piece since neither of the later dark greens were ever used in conjunction with blanks from what is often referred to as the "Nearcut era." To avoid confusion, it is highly recommended when referring to this early dark green that it be called Early Dark Emerald to avoid confusion with the two later colors of the same name. Production of Early Dark Emerald seems to have ceased prior to 1920 and may have been produced for only one or two years.

Also seen in the opposing color plate are Early Cobalt (aka Early Royal Blue) and Early Ebony, two colors discussed elsewhere, and a red flashed piece. The latter does not represent colored glass; rather the color is imparted by applying it to the surface of a colorless piece. Beginning collectors sometimes confuse flashed pieces with true colored glass but with a little experience such items become quite easy to recognize.

Row 1
1) Early Dark Emerald #2780 Strawberry ½ gallon tall tankard jug, gold encrusted, signed "NEARCUT." $250.00.
2) Ebony #2351 punch bowl with Crystal foot. $650.00 set.
3) Crystal #2760 Daisy ½ gallon tall tankard jug, red flashed with gold trim, signed "NEARCUT." $400.00.

Row 2
1) Early Dark Emerald #2766, 4" nappy, gold encrusted, signed "NEARCUT." $25.00.
2) Early Dark Emerald #2766, 9" nappy, gold encrusted, signed "NEARCUT." $75.00.
3) Early Dark Emerald #2658, 4 ounce souvenir mug, signed "NEARCUT." $40.00.
4) Early Dark Emerald Lotus 9" nappy. $150.00.

Row 3
1) Ebony #2729, 6" nappy, bottom view. $125.00.
2 – 5) Early Cobalt #2635 Fernland four piece toy table set. $175.00 set.
6) Early Cobalt #2631 Marjorie 5" nappy, signed "NEARCUT." $125.00.

Row 4
1) Early Dark Emerald #2766 Thistle creamer, signed "NEARCUT." $60.00.
2) Early Dark Emerald #2766 Thistle spooner, signed "NEARCUT." $60.00.
3) Early Dark Emerald #2766 Thistle tumbler, signed "NEARCUT." $35.00.
4) Early Dark Emerald #2766 Thistle ½ gallon jug, signed "NEARCUT." $175.00.

Plate 2

Carnival glass results from the treatment of hot glass with a spray of metallic salts which produces a very pleasing iridescent effect. Cambridge first used this treatment in 1908, preceded only by Fenton Art Glass Company, circa 1907. Cambridge also produced carnival glass circa 1916 – 1917. At the time, the ware was called iridized or iridescent glass. Carnival is a name given to this type of decoration by collectors.

Carnival glass is included in this book on Cambridge colors due to its color appearance and the fact that much carnival glass required a colored base to produce the final array of colors.

The iridizing treatment was used on items from many of the major Nearcut lines and many pieces are signed "NEARCUT." Cambridge carnival is found in four color classifications. These are Marigold on Crystal blanks, Green on Emerald blanks, Blue on Early Dark Cobalt blanks, and Purple on Mulberry blanks.

This is a crossover collectible with both carnival collectors and Cambridge collectors eagerly seeking out the relatively scarce supply.

Row 1
1) #2780 Strawberry 8" nappy, E shape, Mulberry blank, signed "NEARCUT." $250.00.
2) #2651 Feather handled custard, Emerald blank. $100.00.
3) #2651 Feather punch bowl, Emerald blank, signed "NEARCUT." $2000.00.
4) #2651 Feather spooner, Crystal blank, signed "NEARCUT." $300.00.
5) #2651 Feather creamer, Mulberry blank, signed "NEARCUT." $250.00.

Row 2
1) #2340 lamp base or vase, Emerald blank. $750.00.
2) #2780 Strawberry celery, Early Cobalt blank, signed "NEARCUT."*
3) #2780 Strawberry 4" nappy, Mulberry blank, signed "NEARCUT." $50.00.
4) #2780 Strawberry 9½" low footed bowl, Crystal blank, signed "NEARCUT." $400.00.
5) #2351 handled custard, Emerald blank. $125.00.

Row 3
1) #2780 Strawberry creamer, Mulberry blank, signed "NEARCUT." $250.00.
2) #2675 Buzz Saw two ounce perfume, Emerald blank. $450.00.
3) #2766 Thistle spooner, Crystal blank, signed "NEARCUT." $350.00.
4) #2780 Strawberry puff box, Crystal blank. $150.00.
5) #2780 Strawberry creamer, Emerald blank, signed "NEARCUT." $300.00.

Row 4
1) #2766 Thistle spooner, Emerald blank, signed "NEARCUT." $250.00.
2) #2635 Fernland ½ gallon tall tankard, Crystal blank, pastel Marigold carnival.*
3) #2660 Wheat Sheaf six ounce tall cologne, Emerald blank. $600.00.
4) #2699 Buzz Saw ½ gallon jug, Emerald blank, signed "NEARCUT." $250.00.
5) #2699 Buzz Saw eight ounce tumbler, Emerald blank. $45.00.

* Due to the uniqueness of this item, no value is provided.

Plate 3

Cambridge first marketed black glass in January 1916, introducing their version at the 1916 Pittsburgh show. Referred to as Ebony in a May 1916 advertisement, it is a sparkling black of very high density. It shows color (amethyst or red) when held to a very strong light but this is of little or no significance to the collector when attempting to identify a piece as Cambridge.

Trade journals indicate Ebony was a very popular color and as such provided good sales for the company. At the time of its introduction, one trade journal had this to say: "Numbered among the season's new offerings are... a fine array of Ebony Black novelties, flower bowls and flower holder blocks...." Almost two years after its introduction, a trade journal reported: "...the Chicago office has just received from the factory some new samples in black glass flower centers and other decorative pieces." Many of the pieces from this era were decorated with hand-painted flowers.

Ebony was reintroduced in 1922 when it was described in a trade journal as "very black and represents an achievement in this class of glassware." Another reporter's opinion of Cambridge Ebony included this statement: "... are showing a very high grade line of ebony glassware, made in vases, candle sticks, bowls and baskets." Ebony most likely remained in the Cambridge line for the balance of the 1920s but without extensive promotion. By late 1929, Ebony was once again being advertised. One advertisement appeared in the November 1929 issue of *China, Glass and Lamps* in which the main caption read: "Ebony and Crystal is Smart." Part of the advertisement copy read: "Not only is the combination of Ebony and Crystal smart and timely, but CAMBRIDGE shapes give it greater attractiveness and sales value."

Since the color itself does not indicate a production date, other factors indicate when a specific piece was made: the shape of the piece; if decorated, the type of decoration as well as the actual decoration; or if etched, the etching.

Row 1
1, 2) #66, 6" candlesticks. $50.00 pair.
3) #87, 9½" vase, gold trim, iridized. $200.00.
4) #124, 3½" basket, 5½" tall. $65.00.
5) Community #2800/114, 9½" three-footed vase. $100.00.
6) Community #2800, 12" vase. $55.00.
7, 8) Community #2800/17 salt and pepper shakers. $125.00 pair.
9) Atomizer, unidentified etching, gold encrusted. $250.00.

Row 2
1) #710 ink bottle. $100.00.
2) Atomizer, etched #739, white gold encrusted. $500.00.
3) #71, 6" cigarette box, sterling and enamel decoration. $350.00.
4) #206, 1½ ounce perfume, unidentified gold band decoration. $250.00.
5) Prism sign, gold encrusted. $250.00.
6) #432 ram's head 8½" bowl. $150.00.
7) #641 two-piece ash receiver, etched #731. $125.00.
8, 9) #511 "Tombstone" bookends. $200.00 pair.

Row 3
1, 2) #1595, 8" candlesticks. $65.00 pair.
3) #82, 5½" basket, hand-painted enamel decoration #23. $750.00.
4) #134, 4½" ashtray, hand-painted enamel decoration #23. $250.00.
5) Community #2800/92, 10" footed sandwich tray, hand-painted enamel decoration #23. $750.00.
6) #2859, 7" candlestick, hand-painted enamel decoration #23. $150.00.

Row 4
1) #102, 6" bonbon and cover, D/610, gold encrusted. $65.00.
2, 4) #1273, 9½" candlesticks, D/630, gold spash. $100.00 pair.
3) #32, 10½" bowl, D/630, gold splash. $60.00.
5) #169 three-piece mayonnaise set, unidentified fuchsia etching, gold encrusted. $100.00.

Plate 4

Azurite, the first of the 1920s opaques, is a light blue opaque color that is darker than the 1930s Windsor Blue. Additional descriptions of Azurite are found in the trade journal reports of its introduction that follow.

Azurite was introduced to the trade in early January 1922 at the Pittsburgh show. "A new shade of colored glassware, which has been the cause of much favorable comment is the 'Azurite' introduced for the first time by the Cambridge Glass Co. ...It is a full-body blue not unlike Harding Blue. On the gold encrusted 'Azurite' the Cambridge Glass Co. has placed a gold label bearing the wording: 'Cambridge Art Glass, Ohio, U.S.A.' " *China, Glass and Lamps*, January 23, 1922. Two months later, another writer described Azurite in this manner: "Of first consideration is 'Azurite,' a sky blue glass of a most odd and attractive solid color. Vases, bowls, comports, candlesticks, etc. are some of the items of this popular line, which also comes in gold encrustations with various decorations and also with a brown iridescent finish." In a late January 1920 trade advertisement, Cambridge itself had this to say about Azurite: "Buyers welcomed this new colored glass at the Pittsburgh exhibit with large orders. The interesting shapes and the stately decorations and gold encrustations appealed to all."

Azurite and Windsor Blue are not confused since Windsor Blue was used primarily with the 1930s Sea Shell line and Azurite pieces will be from the 1920s lines. In addition to the brown iridescent finish mentioned in the trade journal article, Azurite is found with a similar finish in green and purple and possibly other colors.

Row 1
1) Chelsea #172, 6¾" comport, black exterior finish. $150.00.
2) #164, 10" trumpet vase. $125.00.
3) #79, 9" vase, etched Peacock, black enamel encrusted. $2,000.00.
4) Chelsea #130, 10" vase. $150.00.
5) #86, 8" footed vase, D/185, green enamel encrusted. $750.00.
6) Community #2800/235 ewer (wash set pitcher). $850.00.
7) #21, 3½ ounce sherbet. $75.00.

Row 2
1) Community #2800/234 sponge dish and drainer (not visible). $300.00.
2) Doorknob set. $200.00.
3) #215 spittoon. $500.00.
4) #91, 10" stick vase. $75.00.
5) #62 tall comport, 7¼" across, purple exterior finish. $85.00.
6, 7) #70, 8" candlesticks. $75.00 pair.

Row 3
1, 4) #67 Doric column 9½" candlesticks. $150.00 pair.
2) #432 ram's head bowl. $250.00.
3) Community #2800/235 pomade box, gold trim. $75.00.
5) Cologne, etched Dresden, gold encrusted. $500.00.
6) #2899, 2½" flower block. $75.00.
7) Community #2800/244 humidor, metal cover. $250.00.
8, 9) #20 sugar and creamer. $75.00 set.
10) #206, 1½ ounce perfume, unidentified etching, gold encrusted. $350.00.

Row 4
1) Community #2800/234 soap dish and cover. $400.00.
2) Community #2800/234 brush vase. $100.00.
3) #124, 3½" basket, gold trim. $85.00.
4) #158 eight ounce marmalade, Crystal cover. $200.00.
5) #212 matchbook holder. $100.00.
6, 7) Community #2800/235, 7½" candlesticks. $75.00 pair.
8) Community #2800/235 puff box, hand-painted enamel decoration #23. $250.00.
9) #244, 10½" service plate, etched #619, gold encrusted (D/619). $125.00.
10) #301 bitters bottle, etched #619, gold encrusted (D/619). $125.00.

Plate 5

Primrose Yellow was introduced in 1923 and probably was produced for not more than two years. Primrose Yellow is an opaque yellow of considerable warmth and volume. It was described in a trade journal article thusly: "The Primrose Yellow is just what the name implies, a yellow of warmth and volume but not extreme." A subsequent trade journal article had this to say about Primrose Yellow: "...is indeed a striking color. It is made in a complete line, comprising bowls, compotes, candlesticks, vases, etc., decorated with blue, green and black edges or with an Egyptian key border of combined gold and black. The latter decoration is striking and it stands out wonderfully in contrast to the bright yellow."

The beginning collector, prior to seeing known examples of both colors, might confuse Ivory with Primrose Yellow, thinking perhaps a piece of Ivory was in fact Primrose Yellow. Ivory is a very pale cream color while Primrose Yellow is, without question, almost the color of yellow mustard. Once having seen both colors, there should be no problem distinguishing between them.

In its advertising, Cambridge used the name Primrose Yellow rather than just Primrose. Hence, the correct name for this color is Primrose Yellow. Most collectors, however, simply refer to it as Primrose.

Row 1
1) #206 1½ ounce perfume, gold trim. $250.00.
2) 7" deep comport, 8" tall. $85.00.
3) #82, 10" vase, unidentified gold and black decoration. $250.00.
4) #769, 12" vase. $200.00.
5) #78, 10" vase, etched #619, gold encrusted (D/619). $125.00.

Row 2
1) #96 half pound candy jar and cover. $75.00.
2, 3) Community #2800/235, 7" candlesticks, gold trim. $75.00 pair.
4) #307 3" vase, crimped. $60.00.
5) #308, 4¾" ball vase. $75.00.
6) Plymouth #2630 sherbet. $125.00.
7) Atomizer, etched #519, black enamel encrusted, gold trim. $500.00.

Row 3
1) #169 three piece mayonnaise set. $85.00.
2) #64, 5¼" low comport. $40.00.
3,5) #68 10" candlesticks, unidentified black and gold decoration. $250.00 pair.
4) #4, 7¾" bowl, unidentified black and gold decoration. $125.00.

Row 4
1) #31, 9" bowl, etched #2011, black enamel and gold encrusted. $100.00.
2) #124, 3½" basket, 5" tall. $85.00.
3) Ringtree. $150.00.
4) 11½" dresser tray. $75.00.
5) #119, 7" wide basket, 10" tall, black enamel trim. $300.00.

Plate 6

Helio, introduced in January 1923, is an opaque color of the purple family. From a trade journal article of the time comes this description: "Helio is the name of an exceptionally attractive color. It is of the purple family but delicate in tone and very rich in appearance. The shapes in this color are extensive in number and there is a choice of decorations as wide as that in the Azurite and Primrose Yellow." Another column, a week after the preceding, had this to say about Helio: "...a deep shade of lavender, another very attractive color...has been treated with a decoration absolutely new to the trade. This is in the form of white gold, which gives a much finer finish than silver and does not tarnish."

A fair amount of variation in depth of color is found between pieces, but in general, the color is consistent within a given piece. Helio was produced for a short time, probably no more than two years since trade journals make no mention of the color after 1924.

Collectors have used the name Heliotrope to identify this color, but it is not found in any trade reference or Cambridge advertising and should not be used.

Row 1
1) #82, 10" vase, sterling silver decoration.* $600.00.
2) #119, 7" wide basket, 10" tall. $250.00.
3) Atomizer, paneled, unidentified gold decoration. $200.00.
4) 9½" vase, drilled for lamp. $125.00.
5) #72, 7" candlestick. $35.00.
6) #206, 1½ ounce perfume, etched #528 Egypt, gold encrusted. $350.00.
7) #85, 10" footed vase, etched Classic, white gold encrusted. $400.00.

Row 2
1) #45, 9½" low footed comport, etched #2011, gold encrusted. $100.00.
2, 4) #67, 9½" Doric column candlesticks. $150.00 pair.
3) #432, 8½" ram's head bowl, white gold trim. $250.00.
5) #301, 6" vase. $75.00.

Row 3
1) #206, 1½ ounce perfume, enamel flowers. $500.00.
2) Doorknob. $100.00.
3) Atomizer, etched #405, gold encrusted. $400.00.
4) #117, 4½" oval ashtray. $75.00.
5) #14, 10" bowl, on ebony base (plateau). $60.00.
6) Community #2800/235 soap dish and cover. $400.00.
7) #199 one ounce perfume, etched #703, gold encrusted. $350.00.
8) #307, 3" vase, crimped, etched #619, gold encrusted (D/619). $100.00.

Row 4
1, 3) Community #2800/235 pomade boxes, gold trim. $75.00 each.
2) Community #2800/235 puff box and cover, gold trim. $100.00.
4) 11½" dresser tray. $75.00.
5) Community 2800/235, 3¾" pin tray, signed. $75.00.
6) #135, 12" cheese and cracker set. $75.00.
7) #304, 5¾" vase, white gold splash decoration. $100.00.

*Decoration not done by Cambridge.

Plate 7

Ivory is a light cream-colored opaque glass very similar in appearance to the material from which its name was derived. The light hue of this color made it an ideal background base for many of the applied decorations utilizing colored enamels and gold which were popular during the mid-1920s.

The Cambridge Glass Company's cover advertisement for the January 7, 1924, issue of *China, Glass and Lamps* read: "CAMBRIDGE ART GLASS GOLD ENCRUSTED. Your anticipation of the beauty and decorative possibilities of Cambridge Art Glass, Gold Encrusted, will be more than fulfilled in our display during the Pittsburgh Exhibit in January. We invite inspection of our lines of Cambridge Art Glass, plain and decorated crystal and numerous other items...."

An article in this same issue had a section captioned "SOME NEW ITEMS IN DECORATED COLORED GLASSWARE" and was illustrated by a photograph of four pieces of Cambridge ware. It went on to read: "A few of the 1924 offerings in art glass from the Cambridge Glass Co. present a fitting example of the artistic progress of American glass manufacturers.... The Cambridge Glass Co., from its factory at Cambridge, Ohio, during the past three years has sent out a very extensive line of colored glass, specializing on colored glass with gold encrustations. The items shown are some of the new wares. The colors must be seen because they cannot be described.... In the production of the decorated vase basket, artistic heights have been reached. The glass is Ivory in color and the shape is most pleasing...."

The last mention of Ivory in the trade journals occurred in late August and early September 1926 in conjunction with the No. 701 glass place card. Described as a "novelty at a popular price which is bound to be popular and to replace the cardboard place cards on the tables of up-to-date hostesses. Center is etched for writing in name...supplied in Amber-Glo, Emerald, Peach-Blo, Blue Bell and Ivory."

It should be noted that many glass collectors call glass in this color custard glass and even a few glass manufacturers referred to their wares in the color as custard glass. This is not a name used by Cambridge and Cambridge collectors should refer to the color by its company name, Ivory.

Row 1
1) Wetherford 8" nappy. $125.00.
2) #512 Rose Lady figure flower holder, 9½" tall, enamel and silver decorated. $1,250.00.
3) #118, 8" wide basket, 13" tall. $300.00.
4) #25 eight ounce syrup and cover, black enamel trim. $250.00.
5) Block Optic 10" vase. $150.00.

Row 2
1) #244, 10½" service plate, etched Willow, blue enamel encrusted. $400.00.
2) #157 seven ounce footed marmalade, Crystal cover, unidentified black enamel decoration, $300.00.
3) #206, 1½ ounce perfume, etched Dresden, enamel encrusted. $500.00.
4) Perfume, unidentified enamel decoration. $450.00.
5) Blown deep bowl, etched Dresden, enamel encrusted, gold trim. $600.00.

Row 3
1) #206, 1½ ounce perfume, D/630 gold splash. $300.00.
2) #305, 5¾" vase, etched #619, gold encrusted (D/619). $100.00.
3) #86, 8" footed vase, etched Classic, gold encrusted. $300.00.
4) Perfume, unidentified enamel decoration. $450.00.
5) #80, 6" vase, unidentified enamel decoration. $250.00.
6) #83, 8" vase, unidentified enamel decoration. $300.00.
7) #517 "Draped Lady" figure. $350.00.

Row 4
1) #109 Stratford 9½" dolphin candlestick. $250.00.
2) Atomizer, etched #710 and butterflies, gold encrusted. $650.00.
3) 10" comport (top view), unidentified etching, gold and enamel encrusted. $750.00.
4) #510 Temple jar, on ebony base (plateau), etched Willow, blue enamel encrusted. $1,250.00.

Plate 8

Introduced in 1924, Jade is a medium blue-green opaque whose shading tends heavily toward the blue side of the spectrum. It has been described as being similar in color to high quality, old turquoise. Similar to some of the other opaques, from time to time it is found with a slag line. This is a glassmaker's term for a light colored (sometimes almost white) streak through a piece.

Only one reference to Jade was found in the trade journals and it was dated January 7, 1924. "Two new colors in art glass are shown. The footed vase [#2366 vase] is in jade green. The glass is blown and the coloring is as near to jade as glass might be...."

Based on the lack of advertising and general trade comments, plus the relative scarcity of Jade pieces, it would appear Jade was not in production for more than one or two years, if that long.

Row 1
1) #244, 10½" service plate. $50.00.
2) #86, 8" footed vase, etched Classic, gold encrusted. $250.00.
3) "Geisha" figure, 10", one hair bun.*
4) #556, 8" plate, etched #705, gold and enamel encrusted. $150.00.

Row 2
1) #433, 8⅜" plate, embossed Laurel. $50.00.
2) Perfume, gold trim. $250.00.
3) #57, 8¼" footed bowl (comport). $50.00.
4) Perfume lamp, metal base, etched Dragon, black enamel encrusted. $1,250.00.
5) #86, 8" footed vase, white gold splash decoration. $85.00.

Row 3
1) Atomizer, etched #725, gold encrusted. $500.00.
2) Pousse cafe (made from perfume mold). $125.00.
3) 9½" candlestick/vase, etched #725, white gold encrusted. $45.00.
4) #301, 6" vase. $75.00.
5) 9⅜" candlestick, etched #619, white gold encrusted. $50.00.
6) #307, 3" vase, crimped. $75.00.
7 #206 1½ ounce perfume, etched #528 Egypt, gold encrusted. $350.00.

Row 4
1) #39, 11½" bowl, flat rim. $50.00.
2, 3) 8¼" twist candle sticks. $65.00 pair.
4) #30, 10" bowl, etched #705, gold and enamel encrusted. $300.00.

*Due to the uniqueness of this item, no value is provided.

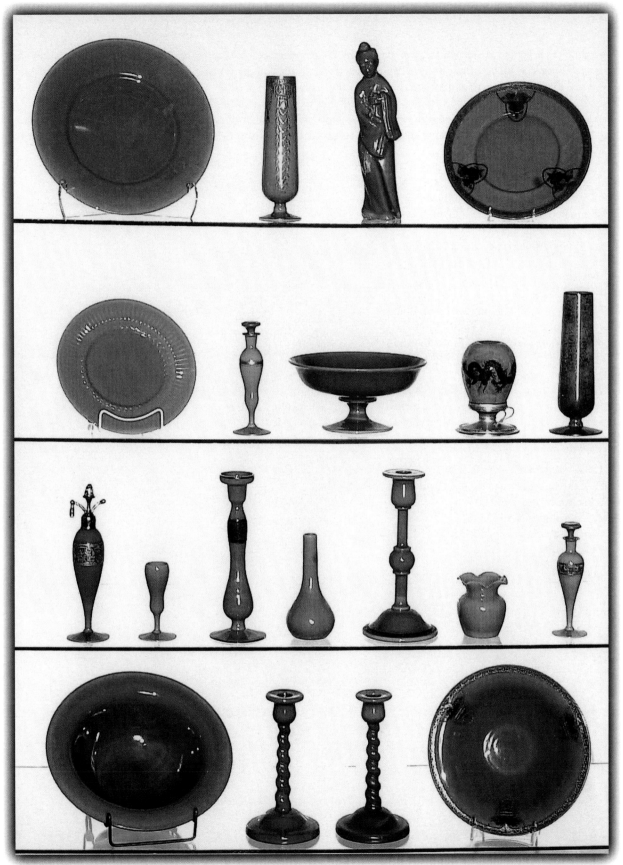

Plate 9

23

Avocado, a rich yellow green opaque, was named by collectors since no Cambridge name has ever been authenticated. There is very limited evidence it might have been, at least within the company, called Pomona Green. The collector-assigned name evolved due to the color's similarity to the flesh of the avocado.

No reference to the color has been found in the trade journals or Cambridge advertising. Even if it proved to be an unpopular color, the fact that no mention of its initial appearance in the Cambridge showrooms is somewhat of a mystery.

Due to the shapes found, most Cambridge experts agree the color is from the 1926 – 1928 time period and was produced for only a very short time.

Row 1
1, 2) #437, 9½" candlesticks. $100.00 pair.
3) #3085 nine ounce goblet, optic. $250.00.
4) #124, 68 ounce jug. $600.00.
5) Round Line #933 cup and saucer. $125.00.

Row 2
1) #394 ice tub. $250.00.
2) #3085, 2½ ounce footed tumbler, optic. $125.00.
3) #414 humidor and cover. $650.00.
4) #3085, 4½ ounce claret, optic. $150.00.

Row 3
1) #732, 12" four footed refractory bowl, etched Dresden Rose, gold encrusted. $450.00.
2) #3085 five ounce footed tumbler, optic, etched #527, gold encrusted. $250.00.
3, 4) #511 "Tombstone" bookends, etched Dresden Rose, gold encrusted. $500.00 pair.

Row 4
1) #381, 8½" soup plate. $75.00.
2) #639, 4½" candlestick, etched #527, gold encrusted. $60.00.
3) #710 pen tip holder. $100.00.
4) #902, 13½" oval tray. $125.00.
5) #710 pen and pencil holder. $150.00.

Plate 10

Carrara is a brilliant, full-bodied white opaque that shows considerable opalescence on the edges or in thinner sections when held to a strong light. The scarcity of representative pieces in this color would indicate that it is the least common of the opaque colors. Carrara was used in a very limited number of patterns with the Community line found the most often.

Based on a comment in a trade journal article dating to May 1922, it appears that Carrara was introduced in the spring of 1922. "...Another line which is attracting a good deal of attention is the company's 'Carrara' ware in translucent white and encrusted gold, comprising a variety of items which form the fancy lines, with bowls obtainable with ebony glass bases." The following January, a trade journal article would lead the reader to believe Carrara was newly introduced: "Leading the offerings in colored glassware and the color runs clear through as it is a body color, are the new Primrose Yellow, Helio and Carrara." This same article went on to say later "The Carrara is a brilliant white and stands in strong contrast to the deep black Ebony."

Carrara was probably produced for not more than two years as there is no mention of it in the trade journals after 1923.

Royal Blue is a transparent dark blue color that was in the Cambridge line almost from the beginning. Named Royal Blue, it was reintroduced in January 1916 as a new color. Production seems to have been sporadic over the next 10 – 12 years with little promotion or advertising. Blanks from the 1920s are known in this dark blue color but there are no specific references to Royal Blue to be found in the trade journals from this time period. Apparently production had ceased by the late 1920s and the name lay dormant until 1931 when the color was reintroduced. The early color is often referred to as Early Royal Blue to distinguish it from the later color.

Amberina is a seldom seen color from the 1920s. No trade journal references have been found and examples of this color will be found in very few collections. The name Amberina is used here but there is no indication this is a name used by Cambridge.

Row 1
1) Amberina #52, 7" footed vase.*
2) Royal Blue #206, 1½ ounce perfume, etched #610, gold encrusted. $300.00.
3, 5) Royal Blue #550, 10 ounce lemonade mug, wide optic, etched #703, white gold encrusted. $75.00 each.
4) Royal Blue tankard footed jug, wide optic, etched #703, gold encrusted. $300.00.

Row 2 Carrara
1) #63, 6" wide comport, unidentified etching, gold encrusted. $125.00.
2) Community #2800/235 puff box, unidentified gold and enamel decoration. $250.00.
3) 7½" wide comport. $100.00.
4) Doorknob, plain top. $50.00.
5) Feather #2651 ruffled sundae/comport.*

Row 3 Carrara
1, 2) Community #2800/235, 7½" candlesticks, black enamel trim. $125.00 pair.
3) Doorknobs, polished tops. $125.00 set.
4) #47, 6½" comport, unidentified enamel decoration, gold trim. $400.00.

*Due to the uniqueness of this item, no value is provided.

Plate 11

27

Introduced some time during the first four months of 1923, Topaz is a yellow-green transparent color, a color which is often called "vaseline" because of its similarity to the color of a popular brand of petroleum jelly. Glass collectors, as a whole, have lumped together any glass of this color, regardless of the maker, into a category called "Vaseline Glass." Cambridge never used that name or described its color in such a manner.

Topaz was not mentioned in trade journal articles describing the Cambridge ware seen at the January 1923 Pittsburgh exhibit. The first trade journal reference occurred in May 1923. Topaz was also shown at the 1924 exhibit based on this trade journal comment dated January 14, 1924: "There is a very complete line of mulberry, topaz and emerald glass, of candle sticks, jugs, bowls, tumblers and stemware that is colorful and interesting." A May 1925 trade journal article describing what was then available at Cambridge showrooms made reference to the keg set being available in Topaz. This was the last reference to Topaz found in the trade journals.

Production of Topaz resumed, probably for a short time, after the October 1931 introduction of the Statuesque line since pieces from this line with Topaz bowls are known. Pieces from other lines dating to this same time period are also known in Topaz and are further evidence for production of the color during the 1930s.

Row 1
1, 2) 10" dolphin candlesticks, dome foot.*
3) Samovar, metal mounts, etched Adams. $500.00.
4) Oriental figure, two hair buns, 9½". $450.00.

Row 2
1) Perfume. $150.00.
2) Stratford #5 two pint jug, signed. $250.00.
3) #1018 loaf sugar cube tray. $100.00.
4) Caprice #1, 10 ounce goblet.*
5) #3115 nine ounce goblet, Topaz bowl, Willow Blue stem and foot, etched #731. $75.00.
6) #299, 5" candy box, three footed. $100.00.

Row 3
1) Perfume. $100.00.
2) #112, 5" open edge plate. $150.00.
3) #112, 4½" open edge nappy. $150.00.
4) #7801 five ounce roemer, Topaz bowl, Crystal stem and foot. $50.00.
5, 7) #3400 ball shape salt and pepper shakers, metal lids. $75.00 pair.
6) Statuesque 3011/9 three ounce cocktail, Crown Tuscan stem and foot. $650.00.
8) Door knobs. $200.00 set.

Row 4
1) #31, 9" bowl. $65.00.
2) #520 Buddha figure on cast metal lamp. $450.00.
3) #30, 10" bowl, etched #707, gold encrusted. $125.00.

* Due to the uniqueness of this item, no value is provided.

Plate 12

Mulberry was introduced in 1923 and is a medium to deep shade of amethyst. It has been described as a "rather dull transparent color, not showing the sparkling beauty found in the later Amethyst."

Mulberry's first reference in the trade journals came in May 1923: "An extensive line of salad plates in colored glass recently has been added to the line of the Cambridge Glass Co. The plates come in Azurite, Ebony, Helio, Primrose Yellow, and in the new shades of topaz, light green and mulberry...In stemware the Cambridge line has been increased by additions in colored glass. The new shades are topaz, light green and mulberry. The most wanted shapes come in the new colors...." Later that same year another trade journal reported "In transparent colors new things in emerald, mulberry and topaz include the popular items in the fancy lines, such as console sets, jugs, plates, comports, and stemware...." Mulberry continued to be mentioned in the trade journals through 1925. No further mention is found, probably indicating it was not offered in 1926 or later.

A problem that may be encountered with Mulberry is that there appears to have been an earlier color, also referred to as mulberry. A June 1916 trade journal article referenced "a new glass called 'Mulberry' in a number of specialities." Additional references are dated July 1916 and January 1917, when this appeared: "Important additions have been made to the handsome Mulberry line...." Currently, there are no authenticated examples of this early Mulberry.

Some pieces of the 1923 Mulberry are found with the large "C in a triangle" trademark and any piece so marked will be the 1923 Mulberry. The correct color of an unmarked item can only be determined with a working knowledge of the shapes and production dates during the time period 1916 – 1925. All of the pieces shown on the opposing page are in the 1923 mulberry.

Goldenrod, as the name implies, is a yellow color that could be described as marigold yellow. It is a transparent color that when first seen appears to be a flashed color but upon closer examination reveals itself to be a true colored glass. Goldenrod is seldom seen today and examples will be found in few collections. It may or may not be the same color referred to as "Golden Showers" in a January 1927 trade journal report where it was described as "a golden color in glass, true golden color."

Row 1 Mulberry
1) Community electric lamp. $300.00.
2) #112, 7" open edge plate. $150.00.
3) Boudoir lamp, beaded fringe. $750.00.
4) #525 wide optic footed cocktail shaker, metal lid. $125.00.

Row 2 Mulberry
1) #206, 1½ ounce perfume, ebony fan stopper. $250.00.
2) Perfume. $125.00.
3) #198 perfume. $75.00.
4) #340, 8" handled relish, etched #732. $85.00.
5) #3077 nine ounce goblet. $40.00.
6, 7) Stratford #109, 9½" dolphin candlesticks. $450.00 pair.

Row 3 Mulberry
1) Georgian #319 nine ounce tumbler. $50.00.
2) Cat bottle, eight ounce, satin finish. $85.00
3) #2810 puff box & cover. $75.00.
4) #7606 nine ounce goblet, etched Marjorie, gold encrusted. $250.00.
5) #2798, 3" birthday candlestick. $75.00.
6) #2206 three-piece mayonnaise set. $60.00.

Row 4 Goldenrod
1) Centennial #25, 10¾" bowl. $200.00.
2) Stratford #12 three pint jug, signed. $450.00.
3) Centennial #14, 10" bowl, etched Willow border. $250.00.
4) Decagon #809, 6¼" plate, etched #731, signed. $75.00.

Plate 13

In late spring 1923, Cambridge introduced a light transparent green glass, the color of which they named Emerald. Unfortunately for today's collectors, they had previously used the name for a dark green color some seven years earlier. Twenty-six years later, the name Emerald was used again for another dark green color. Consequently, Cambridge collectors have taken to using the name "Light Emerald" to describe the 1923 color. The color was to remain in the Cambridge line 20 years, but fell victim to World War II and the resulting raw material shortages.

There was very little mention of Emerald in the trade journals. One of the few trade reports was this, dating to May 1923: "An extensive line of salad plates in colored glass recently has been added to the line of the Cambridge Glass Co....The plates come in Azurite, Ebony, Helio, Primrose Yellow, and in new shades of topaz, light green and mulberry....In stemware, the Cambridge line has been increased by additions in colored glass. The new shades are topaz, light green, and mulberry. The most wanted shapes come in the new colors...."

The color was used extensively during the 1920s and 1930s with most lines being produced in Emerald, lines such as Wetherford, Round, Decagon, and 3400, the latter three plain and etched.

In the fall of 1929, a satin finished line was introduced. This was an acid treatment that resulted in the pieces being semi-opaque and a new name was assigned to each color so treated. In the case of Emerald, the name given was Jade Green. In most instances, the complete pattern side of the piece was acid treated. One exception was the La Fleur line where the raised flowers were left unetched or clear, in contrast to the frosted body.

Row 1

1) #3400/27, 67 ounce jug, etched Gloria, gold encrusted. $750.00.
2) #1300, 8" footed vase, Crystal foot, etched Gloria. $175.00.
3) #550, 10 ounce lemonade mug, wide optic, sponged acid treatment around top, etch Dragon, gold encrusted. $650.00.
4) #787, 10" aquaria, etched Imperial Hunt Scene, gold encrusted. $750.00.
5) #3115 nine ounce goblet, Crystal stem and foot, etched #731. $50.00.
6) #3075/6, 80 ounce jug and cover, etched #703, gold encrusted. $300.00.

Row 2

1) Decagon #851 ice pail, signed, etched Apple Blossom. $150.00.
2) #671 two-piece epergne, three sections. $100.00.
3) Aero Optic #782, 8½" vase, etched #717. $125.00.
4) Wetherford individual footed almond. $25.00.
5) Stratford #463, 12" handled dolphin bowl. $200.00.

Row 3

1) #7927½ five ounce hollow stem champagne. $40.00.
2) Decagon #867 creamer, etched Adams, gold encrusted. $30.00.
3) 7" vase or refrigerator jar. $50.00.
4) #681 dresser compact, Peach-blo rose knob, unidentified gold decoration, colonial figures. $125.00.
5) #1069, 11 ounce goblet, Crystal foot. $50.00.

Row 4

1) #124, 68 ounce jug and cover, etched #740. $250.00.
2, 4) Jade Green Decagon #646, 5" candlesticks. $65.00 pair.
3) Jade Green Springtime #1152, 10½" bowl. $85.00.
5) Honeycomb #95 one pound candy jar and lid. $50.00.

Plate 14

Row 1

1) #769, 12" vase, gyro optic, etched Dragon. $950.00.

2) #575 perfume. $75.00.

3) #279, 13" vase, etched #717, rim etched #524, gold encrusted. $250.00.

4) #107, 13 ounce tumbler, etched Portia. $60.00.

5) Cocktail shaker, wide optic, handled footed metal lid, sterling silver boat scene decoration.* $450.00.

6) #198 perfume, sterling decoration.* $125.00.

7) #105, 62 ounce jug, Rockwell sterling silver Oriental scene.* $500.00.

Row 2

1) #3104 five ounce tall hoch, cut Crystal stem. $200.00.

2) Perfume, satin finish, gold trim. $85.00.

3) #1070, 36 ounce pinch decanter, etched #710. $200.00.

4) #124, 3½" basket, 5" tall. $50.00.

5) #507 jar and cover, satin finish, Rockwell sterling silver Oriental scene.* $450.00.

6) #556, 8" plate, etched #732, green enamel encrusted. $40.00.

Row 3

1) 4¼" candlestick, etched #703. $30.00.

2) #674, 13" bowl, signed, etched #732, gold encrusted. $85.00.

3, 4) #136 sugar and creamer, etched #517. $100.00 set.

5) #109, 39 ounce jug, etched Cleo. $250.00.

Row 4

1) #3400/40 sugar shaker, Crystal foot, etched Apple Blossom. $350.00.

2) #612, 6" master nut comport. $40.00.

3) #119, 83 ounce jug, etched Waterlily. $125.00.

4) Tally-Ho #1402/33 sugar. $25.00.

5) #3400/10, 11" handled sandwich tray, etched Apple Blossom, gold and enamel encrusted. $85.00.

*Decoration not done by Cambridge.

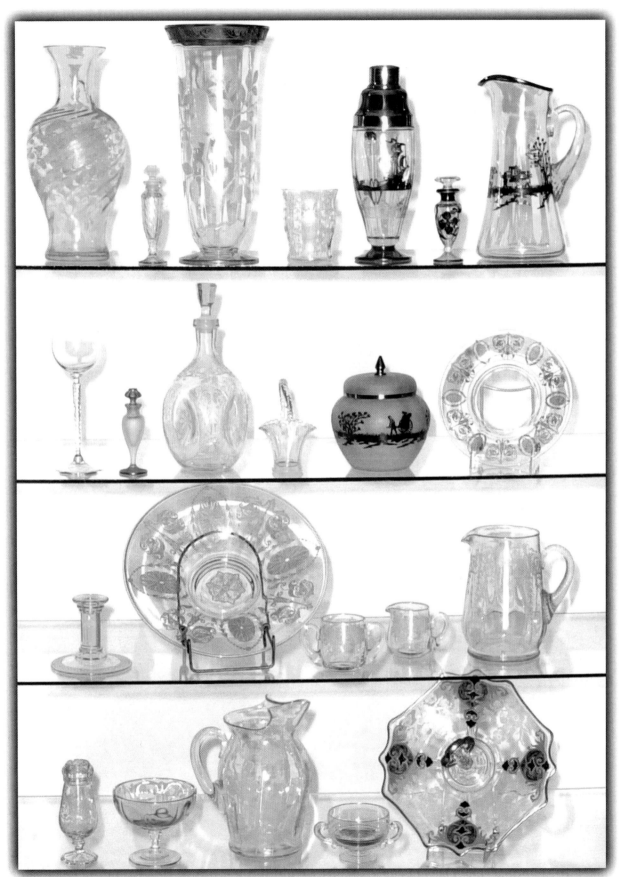

Plate 15

35

Amber made its debut at the 1924 Pittsburgh exhibit. Cambridge Amber is a transparent color, deep brown in tone. A trade journal writer at the time of its introduction described it as: "A new line of amber glass, deep and rich in tone is offered for the first time." The following May a trade journal reporter who had just been to the New York City Cambridge showrooms had this to say: "At the same time the first samples of gold encrusted colored stemware arrived, in cobalt, amber, mulberry and emerald."

For the next two years the trade journals used the name Amber as did Cambridge advertising. In March 1925 the name Amber-Glo started to appear. Whether or not there was a simultaneous formula change or if the name change was strictly a sales tactic remains unclear. According to one trade journal: "Amber Glo, by the way, is a new amber tint of a rich deep hue, and is a color of wonderful warmth and of strong appeal in the many numbers in which it is featured." Amber-Glo continued to appear as a color name in Cambridge advertising until late 1929 when it was replaced with a lighter shade in the same family, it being called Madeira. After about one year, Madeira was discontinued and the deeper shade, once again called Amber, returned to the Cambridge catalog.

As part of their 1929 fall line, Cambridge brought out a satin-finished line of console sets and vases. This line was produced by acid treating only the pattern side of the piece; thus making it semi-opaque. New color names were used for pieces so treated and in the case of Amber the name was Cinnamon.

Madeira is perhaps best described by the original trade journal descriptions. Quoting from an article dated June 17, 1929: "...has recently introduced a light golden amber shade which it has named Madeira. The Madeira is neither a canary yellow nor a deep amber but what might be described as a halfway shade between the two. It is a clear, entrancing color and keeps its tone effect in both blown and pressed ware." During the summer of 1929, Cambridge advertisements featuring the Cleo etching on Decagon blanks stated the line was available in Madeira as well as the other prevailing transparent colors. A February 1930 trade journal article references Madeira, while an August 1930 Cambridge advertisement listing available colors, made no mention of Madeira but did include the name Amber.

Row 1 Amber
1) Tankard jug, footed, wide optic. $75.00.
2, 4) Stratford #109, 9½" dolphin candlesticks. $200.00 pair.
3) 12" dolphin, full handled bowl, wide optic.*
5) #14 handled decanter, etched Imperial Hunt Scene, gold encrusted. $500.00.

Row 2 Amber
1) #95 one pound candy jar, wide optic, gold trim. $75.00.
2, 3) #1595, 8" candlesticks. $60.00 pair.
4) #3085 nine ounce goblet, etched Imperial Hunt Scene, gold encrusted. $125.00.
5) #510 temple jar, Ebony cover, on Ebony plateau (base), etched #703, gold encrusted. $200.00.
6) #206, 1½ ounce perfume, etched Wild Rose. $150.00.
7) #803 batter jug, etched Cleo. $200.00.

Row 3 Amber
1) Turtle planter.*
2) Wetherford perfume. $75.00.
3) #805 syrup, lid, and liner. $75.00.
4) #710 letter holder, etched Dresden Rose, gold encrusted. $100.00.
5) #531, 7½" wide, tall comport, etched #720, gold encrusted. $75.00.
6) #198 perfume, gold silk screen decoration. $100.00.

Row 4 Madeira
1) #2899, 5" flower block. $40.00.
2) #3051 nine ounce goblet, narrow optic. $20.00.
3) #3400/55 cream soup, signed, etched Brettone. $30.00.
4) #3122 nine ounce goblet, etched Diane. $75.00.
5) Tally-Ho #1402/8 five ounce low stem juice. $15.00.
6) Decagon #597, 8⅜" salad plate, signed. $8.00.
7) #3077 nine ounce goblet, etched Cleo. $30.00.

*Due to the uniqueness of this item, no value is provided.

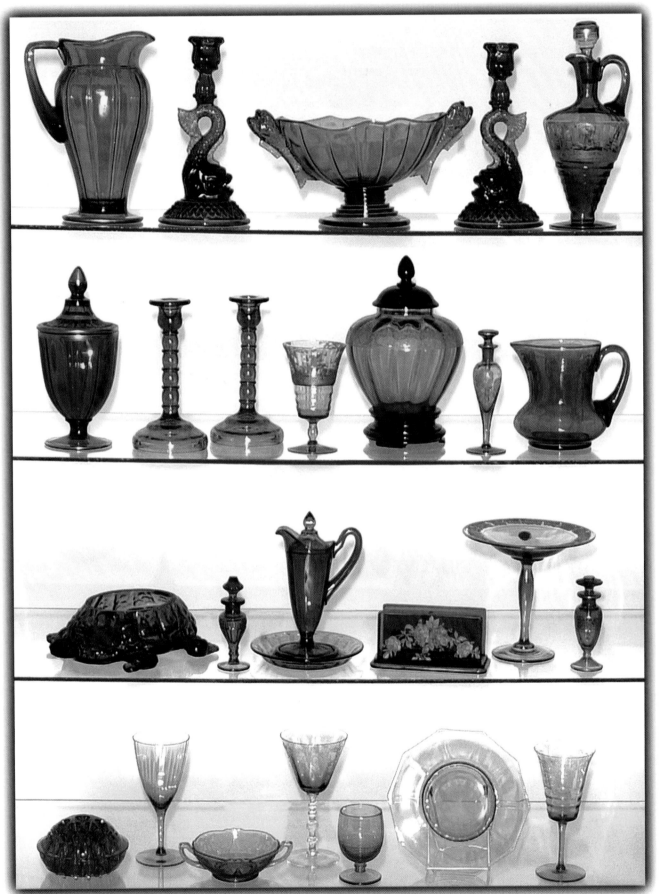

Plate 16

Blue I — Beginning in the mid-1920s and continuing through the early 1930s, Cambridge produced glass in several blue colors that are problematic for today's collectors. The first trade journal reference to a blue during this time period came in April 1924: "Another color which seems to have quite general popularity is cobalt blue, which is shown both plain and with encrustations of white and yellow gold, in a wide range of pieces and shapes." In September of that year another trade journal article contained this statement: "...and in transparent colors of aurora blue, amber, amethyst, topaz and mulberry." Whether "aurora blue" was a Cambridge name or a descriptive term used by the writer remains an unanswered question. November 1924 saw a trade journal report of refreshment sets in "blue, green and amethyst," these sets being decorated with gold encrusted mah jong tiles. Collectors have designated this blue "Blue I." It is medium blue, darker than either Willow Blue or Moonlight but lighter than Ritz Blue. It has been reported that Blue I is highly fluorescent under black light. Blue I exhibits significant gathering effect, thus appearing darker in thick sections of glass or in overall heavier pieces.

Trade journal references to "blue" continued for the next several years. Some collectors believe there is another distinct blue color, a color designated Blue II. It has been reported such pieces react only slightly under black light. However, visually it is difficult, if not impossible, to categorize pieces into two distinct color groupings.

Ritz Blue — In October 1929, Cambridge informed its agents that it had just produced a new color known as Ritz Blue. The announcement described it as "a most rich shade of blue and if anything you might call it somewhat delicate, as it is not a harsh color, as blue is generally considered." The announcement went on to say that color was being used to produce a small line that included 3077 stemware, a luncheon set from the Decagon line, and a few accessory items. It has been reported that Ritz Blue shows no reaction when exposed to black light. Ritz Blue remained in the Cambridge line for at least two years, appearing in a 1931 advertisement. Ritz Blue is identified by the blank since evidence indicates the other dark transparent blues were discontinued prior to the introduction of 3077 stemware and the Decagon line.

Row 1 Blue I
1) #107, 22 ounce overnite jug and cover, crackle. $200.00.
2) Chelsea #47, 8¼" deep bowl, cut #4061. $85.00.
3) Perfume. $125.00.
4) #106, 66 ounce jug and cover, etched mah jong tiles, gold encrusted. $400.00.

Row 2 Blue I
1) #1 keg set, Ebony top, metal frame and spigot. $300.00.
2) #447 two-piece mayonnaise set, unidentified floral cut. $65.00.
3) #124, 3½" basket, 5" tall. $75.00.
4) #441, 10½" low footed bowl or comport. $45.00.

Row 3 Ritz Blue
1, 2) Decagon #979 sugar and creamer, signed. $45.00 set.
3) #394 ice tub. $100.00.
4) Decagon #865 cup and saucer, signed. $25.00.
5) Decagon #597, 8⅜" salad plate, signed. $10.00.

Row 4 Ritz Blue
1) Mt. Vernon #2, 6½ ounce tall sherbet. $35.00.
2) Mt. Vernon #5, 8½" salad plate. $25.00.
3) #198, 1½ ounce perfume, etched #517, gold encrusted. $125.00.
4) #206, 1½ ounce perfume, etched #527, gold encrusted. $250.00.
5) #158 footed marmalade, crystal cover. $85.00.
6) Samovar, metal fittings, etched #695. $400.00.

Plate 17

Introduced at the 1925 Pittsburgh exhibit, Rubina is not one color but several. Rubina shades from a red at the top and bottom of an item to a green and then to a medium blue in the middle of the piece. Yellow may also be present in some pieces. Since the final color is achieved by reheating the piece by hand, there is a great variation from piece to piece in the degree of shading and the intensity of the resulting colors.

"In 'Rubina' glass, which can be had both plain and block optic, new shapes in comports, bowls, vases, candlesticks and other pieces have been developed. Especially attractive is the refreshment set in block optic 'Rubina.' The new glass is not one color but a natural three or more tone glass in which the predominating shades are red, green and blue, each tone diverging into the other." The preceding was taken from a trade journal report of new wares for 1925.

A short time later, another trade journal reporter had this to say: "Rubina is a new color used for a full line of stemware and fancy numbers. This shades from blue to a red, like the old fashioned changeable silks, and is very lovely." These are the only known trade journal references to Rubina. All indications are it was offered for only a short time, probably not more than one season; thus it was out of the Cambridge line by 1926.

Row 1
1) Honeycomb tall covered candy. $300.00.
2) Community #2800, 10 ounce goblet, signed. $250.00.
3) Block Optic 10¼" vase. $200.00.
4) #550, 10 ounce lemonade mug, wide optic, signed. $150.00.
5) Tall tankard jug. $750.00.

Row 2
1) #3051 nine ounce goblet, narrow optic. $200.00.
2) #3051, 2½ ounce wine, narrow optic. $200.00.
3) #3051 five ounce cafe parfait, narrow optic. $200.00.
4) #3051, 10 ounce table tumbler, narrow optic. $125.00.
5) #3051, 2½ ounce cocktail, narrow optic. $175.00.
6, 7) #490 oval sugar and creamer. $850.00 set.

Row 3
1, 3) #1630, 12 ounce tumblers, optic. $125.00 each.
2) #107, 76 ounce jug, optic. $600.00.
4) Honeycomb #57, 8¼" footed bowl or comport. $150.00.
5) #83, 8" vase, optic. $225.00.

Row 4
1, 3) Stratford #109, 9½" dolphin candlesticks. $1250.00 pair.
2) Stratford #70, 12" rolled edge bowl. $600.00.
4) Honeycomb 7" comport, unidentified floral etching, gold encrusted. $300.00.

Plate 18

Row 1
1) #119, 7" wide basket, 11" tall. $450.00.
2) Small oval basket made from #490 sugar.*
3) Block Optic 12 ounce tumbler. $125.00.
4) Block Optic #500/122, 56 ounce jug and cover. $750.00.

Row 2
1) Wide optic punch bowl. $1,800.00.
2) Honeycomb 6¼" comport, sponged acid finish. $200.00.
3) #1352 frog vase.*

Row 3
1) #305, 5¾" vase, optic. $200.00.
2) Wide Optic #525 three ounce footed cocktail. $125.00.
3) #432, 8½" ram's head bowl. $850.00.
4) #488 overnite set (jug lid missing). $750.00 set, as is.

Row 4
1, 3) # 438, 8¼" candlesticks. $200.00 pair.
2) Honeycomb #25, 10" bowl. $150.00.
4) #3400/96 two ounce ball-shaped oil. $250.00.
5) Georgian #319 nine ounce tumbler. $200.00.

*Due to the uniqueness of this item, no value is provided.

Plate 19

Introduced during the summer of 1925, Peach-blo is a soft pink with warmth and sparkle. In general, pink is a very hard color to maintain when working a pot of glass and tends to have a considerable amount of variation in density and sparkle. This holds true for Peach-blo.

"...An unusual number of lovely new things have arrived at the show rooms of the Cambridge Glass Co. ...The most important is a new color in glass known as peachblo. It is made up in stemware and in footed and straight sided tumblers in a wide optic and may be had either undecorated or with encrusted band and line treatment. This color is absolutely unique in modern glass. It has the warmth and sparkle of amber and the gayety of Du Barry Rose and is different from these, while combining the charms of both. The name, Peachblo, describes it perfectly." The preceding comes from a column entitled *New York Trade Notes* and first appeared in print August 3, 1925.

As with many other manufacturers, Cambridge used colors in combination. This trend was especially popular in the late 1920s and early 1930s when Peach-blo was at its peak. The collector will find stemware where Peach-blo has been used in conjunction with a color other than Crystal.

In late 1929 Cambridge brought out their Satin Finish Line with one of the early pieces being the 16" No. 28 "buffalo bowl." Later a number of pieces from the Springtime Line were given the same treatment. The pattern side of the piece was acid treated, giving an etched or satin finish. The non-patterned side was left untreated. When Peach-blo pieces were so treated, the resulting color was called Rose Du-Barry.

In 1934 the name Peach-blo was changed to Dianthus Pink with no apparent formula change. No reason for this change has been determined. The time period of the blank and/or etching is the determining factor in assigning the correct color name. As Dianthus Pink, the color remained in the Cambridge line until October 1943.

Row 1
1) #3051 nine ounce goblet, narrow optic, etched Wild Rose. $40.00.
2) Moderne #3300 five ounce high sherbet. $20.00.
3) #2668 two ounce jug (perfume), no stopper, Nearcut era mold. $75.00.
4) #1 keg set, Ebony top, holder, and tray. $250.00.
5) #3140 tall sherbet, crystal stem and foot. $35.00.
6) #3075/10, 63 ounce tankard jug and cover, etched Imperial Hunt Scene, gold encrusted. $500.00.

Row 2
1) Jug, etched #701. $250.00.
2) #157 seven ounce footed marmalade and cover, crackle. $150.00.
3) #3400/39 tall creamer or syrup, Crystal stem and foot, etched Gloria. $175.00.
4) #3400/83 square A. D. cup and saucer, signed, etched Apple Blossom. $150.00.
5) #1070, 36 ounce pinch decanter, etched Imperial Hunt Scene, gold encrusted. $400.00.
6) #3085 six ounce low sherbet, Light Emerald foot, etched Imperial Hunt Scene, gold encrusted. $85.00.
7) #3015 nine ounce goblet, etched Lorna. $40.00.

Row 3
1) #1316, 7" rabbit box and cover, fur detail. $650.00.
2) Perfume, satin finish, gold trim. $85.00.
3) #898, 14½" roast beef tray with #838 mustard and cover, etched #732. $250.00.
4) #206, 1½ ounce perfume, satin interior, etched #517, gold encrusted. $200.00.
5) #119, 83 ounce jug, crackle. $250.00.

Row 4
1) #1054 three compartment candy box and cover, etched #704. $75.00.
2) #3400/4, 12" four-toed bowl, signed, etched Gloria. $100.00.
3) Springtime #745, 4⅛" candlestick. $25.00.
4) #932, 10½" cake or ice cream tray, etched #731. $100.00.

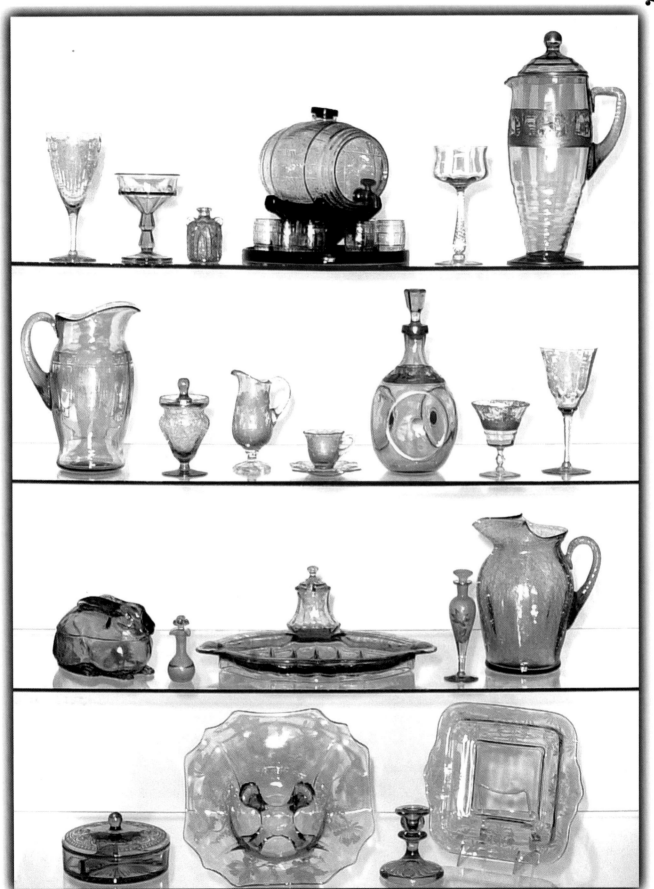

Plate 20

Row 1

1) Tankard jug, paneled, etched Cleo. $600.00.

2) #813 sugar shaker, Crystal lid, etched Cleo. $250.00.

3) #1305, 10" footed globe vase, Crystal stem and foot, etched Apple Blossom. $350.00.

4) #1000, 8" apple plate. $75.00.

5) #1205, 64 ounce jug, Crystal foot, etched Portia. $450.00.

Row 2

1) #3400/38, 80 ounce ball jug, etched Gloria. $500.00.

2) #642 ashtray. $45.00.

3) #3500/26 ram's head 12" fruit basket. $200.00.

4) #1222 turkey with cover. $750.00.

Row 3

1) #3400/150, 12 ounce stein. $45.00.

2) #845 ice bucket (keg). $60.00.

3) #703 flower arranger with #2899, 3" Crystal block. $45.00.

4) #300, 6" three-footed candy box and cover, etched #725, gold encrusted. $75.00.

5) Centennial /Martha Washington #8, 8¼" bowl. $60.00.

Row 4

1) Airplane samovar, brass and wood fittings, satin finish, hand-painted flowers. $1,250.00.

2) Rose Du Barry Decagon #638, 6" three-lite candlestick. $50.00.

3) Springtime #745, 12½" bowl, satin highlights. $75.00.

Plate 21

Blue Bell is a medium dark transparent blue with considerable sparkle. It is sometimes described as being very similar in color to a popular brand of blue-colored commercial glass cleaner. It does exhibit considerable bunching effect and thicker items in this color have a darker appearance than thinner pieces. This variation in appearance is quite apparent in the color plate on the opposing page and is indicative of what is seen when viewing the actual pieces. Some Blue Bell pieces were acid treated to produce a satin finish and this greatly changes the color.

Very little is known about Blue Bell. The earliest trade journal references to Blue Bell date to August and September of 1926. That it is a Cambridge assigned name is proven by its appearance in a Cambridge advertisement on the cover of the August 30, 1926, issue of *China, Glass and Lamps*. The next month it is referenced in an article in the same publication. A year later, in a trade journal article dealing with newly arrived liqueur sets at the New York shows, Blue Bell is again mentioned.

Indications are it was probably in production prior to August and September of 1926. However, its precise production dates remain somewhat of a mystery. The total production period for Blue Bell probably did not originally exceed two years.

A very similar, if not identical, color appears in the 1940s Harlequin sets with the name Tahoe Blue and the reader is referred to that article. The color was produced again during the last years of the original company and once more by the second company. It is not clear if any of this production was actually sold commercially or if it was all experimental and trial runs and under what name, if any, it was produced. See Tahoe Blue and page 85 for illustrations of this later production.

Row 1
1) #513, 13" "Draped Lady" figure flower holder. $1,800.00.
2) Prism sign, gold encrusted. $300.00.
3) #518, 8½" "Draped Lady" figure flower holder. $1,500.00.
4) #396 salt shaker, gold trim. $50.00.
5) Samovar, decanter set, metal frame, hand-painted decoration. $600.00 set.

Row 2
1) Eight ounce dog bottle. $125.00.
2) #3075, 2½ ounce wine, narrow optic. $35.00.
3) #3075, 2½ ounce cocktail, narrow optic. $30.00.
4) #559, 8½" plate, etched #703 Florentine. $30.00.
5, 6) #138 sugar and creamer, etched Willow, gold trim. $300.00 set.

Row 3
1) Springtime #745, 4⅛" candlestick. $45.00.
2) #399 twin salt dip. $40.00.
3) #1315, 5" rabbit box, satin finish. $850.00.
4) #206, 1½ ounce perfume. $100.00.
5) Perfume, etched #704. $125.00.
6) Perfume, etched #704. $100.00.
7, 8) #511 "Tombstone" bookends, etched Dresden Rose, gold encrusted. $250.00 pair.

Row 4
1) #198 perfume, etched #704, gold trim. $100.00.
2) #680 dresser compact, etched #517, gold encrusted. $150.00.
3) Wetherford 4" nappy. $50.00.
4, 5) Stratford #109, 9½" dolphin candlesticks. $500.00 pair.

Plate 22

Willow Blue, a pastel blue color, received considerable attention when it was introduced in the summer of 1928.

"A new color in transparent glass will be shown August 1 [1928] by the Cambridge Glass Co. in its sales and display rooms in New York, Chicago, Boston, Philadelphia and Detroit. The new color from Cambridge is worthy the fullest attention of the trade. The first showing will be made simultaneously in the various show rooms. The new transparent color is called 'Willow Blue'....The color of the new glass is totally different than any now on the market. It is not a deep color, rather it is a strong pastel shade. In the blown pieces, such as goblets, footed tumblers, and so on, the color is rather faint than strong. Pressed ware in the new color, such as plates, bowls and heavy pieces, is free from preponderance of color in one place...shows no bunching." *China, Glass and Lamps,* July 23, 1928.

The Cambridge novice may confuse Willow Blue with Moonlight since both are transparent light blues. For the most part, they can be distinguished by the blank for there is little overlapping of the two colors. Pieces from the Decagon, Round, 3400, and other 1920s and early- to mid-1930s lines will be in Willow Blue, while Moonlight was used primarily with the Caprice and Gyro Optic lines. The one area of overlap was in the Everglade line where early pieces were in Willow Blue and some later production did utilize Moonlight.

In 1929, Cambridge introduced its Satin Finish line, in which pieces were acid treated on the pattern side but not on the reverse or interior. In some instances, highlights of the design were not frosted. Several colors of blanks were used and for each a unique color name was assigned. The resulting color when Willow Blue blanks were used was named Mystic Blue.

For reason or reasons unknown, the name Willow Blue was dropped during the summer of 1933 and the color then became known as Eleanor Blue. Collectors seldom use the latter name, most often referring to it as Willow Blue. Willow Blue/ Eleanor Blue remained in the Cambridge line until 1936 with the debut of Moonlight.

Row 1
1) #84, 12" footed vase, etched Betty, gold trim. $125.00.
2) Tally-Ho #1402/43, 10 ounce tumbler. $25.00.
3) Everglade 13" two-piece oval epergne. $300.00.
4) #3500/90 cigarette holder. $65.00.
5) Moderne #3300, 60 ounce jug. $100.00.

Row 2
1) #3077 nine ounce goblet, unidentified floral cut. $25.00.
2) #955, 62 ounce jug, etched #521. $200.00.
3) #3400/1093 handled relish, etched Apple Blossom. $85.00.
4) Double egg cup. $75.00.
5) #3120 nine ounce goblet, etched #733. $45.00.
6) Decagon #867 sugar, etched #738. $25.00.

Row 3
1) Decagon #867 creamer, etched #738. $25.00.
2) #3130 nine ounce goblet, unidentified floral cut. $30.00.
3) #1506/4, 5" novelty basket, plate shape, signed. $30.00.
4) Decagon #877, 11½" comport, etched #733. $85.00.
5) Martha Washington #30, 80 ounce jug. $125.00.

Row 4
1, 2) Mystic Blue Decagon #638 three-lite candlestick. $150.00 pair.
3) Decagon #611, 2½" individual almond, etched Cleo. $75.00.
4) Martha Washington #45 seven ounce tall sherbet. $25.00.
5) Aero Optic #494 cup and saucer, signed. $20.00.
6) Decagon #878, 4" candlestick, etched #733. $30.00.

Plate 23

51

Introduced in the late summer of 1929, Gold Krystol is a light yellow color with no amber tint. A further description is found in the following trade journal excerpt: "Among the new lines which the Cambridge Glass Co. is offering in blown and pressed stemware for the coming Holiday trade, the newest in stemware is called 'Gold Krystal' in combination of the bowl in the new transparent color — gold — and crystal foot and stem. The transparent shade which gives to 'Gold Krystal' its attractive coloring is an entirely new color with the Cambridge factory. It is light gold and bright and attractive, a close approximation in glass to gold. The coloring holds throughout and it can be distinguished easily. There is no amber tinge to the 'Gold Krystal' of the Cambridge factory. It is rather a deep yellow gold than an amber-gold." *China, Glass and Lamps,* September 1929.

It would seem the writer of the preceding may have mistaken the color name for a line name and at the same time misspelled it. The first time the color name appeared in Cambridge advertising it was spelled Gold Krystol, not Gold Krystal. The writer did correctly observe that the coloring holds throughout; that is, there is no bunching in the heavier areas of the glass.

Gold Krystol remained in the Cambridge line as a major color until the fall of 1943. From then on it was used only for Sea Shell and Stackaway ashtrays until the end of 1952 when that usage also ceased.

Row 1
1) #711, 76 ounce footed jug, etched Gloria. $450.00.
2) #3400, 50 ounce footed jug, etched Gloria. $600.00.
3) #1043, 8½" swan, Style 1, signed. $250.00.
4) #3035 nine ounce goblet, Amber stem and foot, etched Brettone. $75.00.
5) #3025 seven ounce tall sherbet, Amber stem and foot, etched Gloria. $65.00.
6) #1236, 7½" ivy ball, Amber stem and foot. $150.00.

Row 2
1) Double egg cup. $50.00.
2) #3124, 10 ounce goblet, Crystal stem and foot. $35.00.
3) Everglade #23, 5" vase, satin finish. $75.00.
4) Decagon #1090, 7" comport, etched Cleo. $75.00.
5) Decagon #611, 2½" individual almond. $30.00.
6) #3126 nine ounce goblet, Crystal stem and foot. $35.00.
7, 8) #2827 Pansy berry sugar and creamer. $350.00 set.
9) #3123 Aero Optic nine ounce goblet. $40.00.

Row 3
1) Statuesque #3011/9 three ounce cocktail, Crown Tuscan stem and foot. $150.00.
2) #3125 Deauville goblet, Crystal stem and foot, etched Deauville. $60.00.
3) Mt. Vernon #84, 14 ounce stein, signed. $50.00.
4) #3400/97 two ounce ball perfume and 3400/94, 3½" puff box, etched Apple Blossom, brass frames and tray. $450.00 set.
5, 6) #3400/18 salt and pepper shakers, etched Apple Blossom. $100.00 pair.
7) #3104 five ounce tall hoch, Crystal stem and foot. $125.00.
8) #3400/107, 14 ounce stein, Crystal handle. $40.00.

Row 4
1) Decagon #984, 10" handled bowl, signed, etched Lorna. $75.00.
2) Decagon #867 creamer, etched Lorna. $25.00.
3, 4) #3400/16 six ounce footed sugar and creamer, etched Apple Blossom, gold trim. $65.00 set.
5) #3400/38, 80 ounce ball jug, etched Portia, gold encrusted. $500.00.

Plate 24

Carmen, a rich full-bodied red, received its first trade journal mention in February 1931 in what was a review of the Cambridge goods seen at the Pittsburgh exhibit the previous month. Carmen does not have the hardness of appearance or an orange cast often found in reds from other glass companies. The initial trade journal reference described it as "a bright ruby."

One story that has persisted for years is that Cambridge Carmen contains gold as its coloring agent. While it is true that gold or gold compounds can be used to impart a red color to glass, Cambridge did not use gold as its coloring agent. Selenium is another metallic element that will produce a ruby color when added to glass and this is what Cambridge used.

Quoting a trade journal article from June 1931: "...The Cambridge Glass Co.'s dinnerware and stemware in ruby color, which they call 'Carmen,' is among their best sellers. It has been used effectively in many table settings, combined with appropriately decorated china, and since ruby dinnerware is so strikingly different, it has attracted a great deal of favorable attention."

Accompanying an illustration of pieces from the Mount Vernon line was this caption: "...It naturally lends itself to the early American dining room ensemble. The Mount Vernon is made in the finest Cambridge antique colors of amber, royal blue, forest green, carmen and crystal." What made these colors "antique colors" in the writer's mind remains a mystery.

Carmen was the original Cambridge name for their red color. On occasion it was qualified or explained by the word ruby appearing in parenthesis immediately following it. On rare occasion, such as in a trade journal advertisement for the sweet potato vase, the name Ruby appears. There is no indication there was a separate "Ruby" formula and when the name Ruby was used, it appears it was simply a sales tool.

Carmen remained in the Cambridge line until 1943 when it, like so many other colors and lines, was discontinued. Carmen was revived in 1950 but by 1952 its use was greatly reduced and by the fall of 1953, Carmen was not offered on the last price list issued by the original company. The reorganized or second company did produce Carmen colored glassware with no apparent change in the formula.

Row 1
1) Tally-Ho #1402/100 tall sherbet, gold silk screen D/1007/8. $125.00.
2) #1233, 9½" footed vase, etched Rose Point, gold encrusted. $2,500.00.
3) #3500 seven ounce tall sherbet, unidentified gold lion decoration. $100.00.
4) Mt. Vernon #1340, 2½ ounce cologne. $200.00.
5) #3122 nine ounce goblet, etched Diane, gold encrusted. $400.00.
6) #1242, 10" vase, etched Diane, gold encrusted. $1,500.00.

Row 2
1) #1236, 7½" ivy ball, Crystal stem and foot. $85.00.
2 – 6) #3400/119, 12 ounce ball shaped cordial decanter, #1341 one ounce cordials. $85.00 set.
7) #3130 seven ounce tall sherbet, etched #731. $75.00.
8) #3400/92, 2½ ounce tumbler on #3115 Crystal stem and foot. $50.00.
9, 10) #50, 7¾" dolphin candlesticks. $600.00 pair.

Row 3
1) Mt. Vernon #91, 86 ounce jug. $150.00.
2) #1311, 4" footed ashtray, Crystal stem and foot. $75.00.
3) #1067, 11 ounce goblet, Crystal stem and foot. $75.00.
4) #3400/102, 5" globe vase, etched Portia, gold encrusted. $850.00.
5) #3400/851 ice pail, etched Portia, gold encrusted. $1,250.00.

Row 4
1) #306, 3" vase. $65.00.
2, 3) Tally-Ho #1402/80, 6½" candlesticks, gold silk screen D/1007/8. $500.00.
4) Pristine #P569, 9" vase, ruffled. $85.00.
5) #1203 seven ounce old fashioned cocktail, shammed. $25.00.
6) #3104, 3½ ounce cocktail, Crystal stem and foot. $150.00.

Plate 25

The Japonica decoration was one of only several decorations that had its own signature or trademark applied to the piece. The decoration, as well as the trademark, was done in applied white enamel. The Japonica mark is reproduced here somewhat larger than its actual size.

Row 1
1) #1318, 12" footed vase, Crystal stem and foot, D/Japonica, signed with Japonica signature. $3,500.00.
2) # 3400/118, 35 ounce decanter, Crystal stopper. $75.00.
3) Mt. Vernon #38, 13½" candelabrum, Crystal bobeches and prisms. $1,000.00.
4) Tally-Ho #1402/100 one ounce cordial, Crystal stem and foot, sterling silver decoration.* $250.00.
5) #1066 six ounce cafe parfait, Crystal stem and foot. $75.00.
6) #3500/45, 10" footed urn vase, D/Japonica, signed with Japonica signature. $3,500.00.

Row 2
1) #3400/38, 80 ounce ball jug, sterling silver floral decoration.* $850.00.
2) Pristine #P306 candy box and cover. $100.00.
3) #1070, 36 ounce pinch decanter, etched Gloria, silver encrusted. $2,000.00.
4) #1713 cigarette box, four toed, Crystal lid. $125.00.
5) #3400/136, 6" four-toed bowl, fancy edge, D/Japonica. $3,200.00.

Row 3
1, 2) Mt. Vernon #35, 8" candlesticks. $300.00 pair.
3) #1043, 8½" swan, Style III. $300.00.
4) #1192, 6" candlestick, sterling silver decoration.* $150.00.
5) Cambridge Square #3797/26, 11½" plate. $100.00.

Row 4
1) Everglade 10" three-toed bowl, unusual pulled edge. $500.00.
2) #3500/151/1327/925 three-piece A. D. coffee and cordial set, Crystal tray. $150.00.
3) Open "S" edge 7½" square four-footed plate.**
4, 5) Caprice #1338, 6" three-lite candlesticks. **

*Decoration not done by Cambridge.
**Due to the uniqueness of this item, no value is provided.

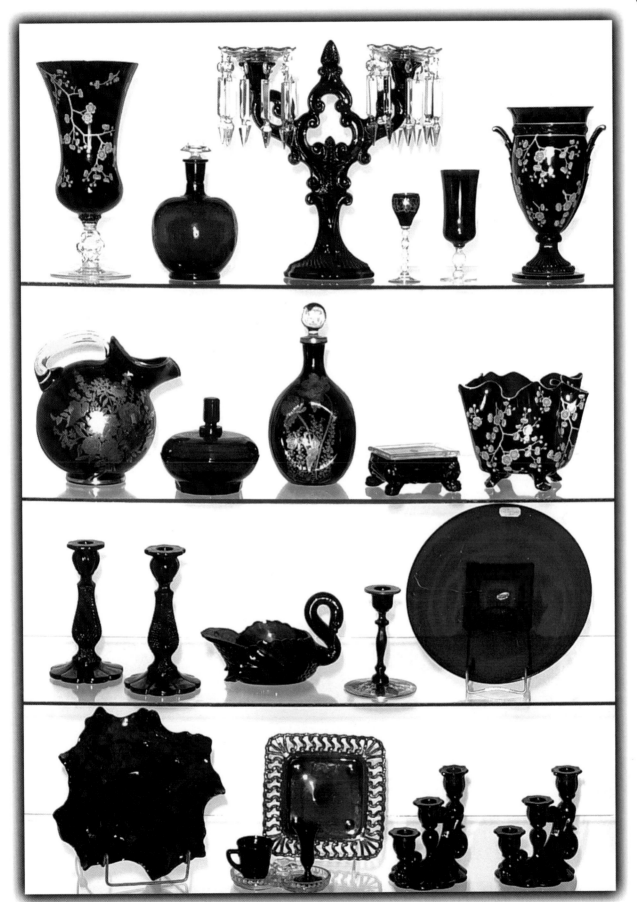

Plate 26

While neither the 1931 *China, Glass and Lamps* trade directory nor the Cambridge-issued 1931 pocket diary mentions Amethyst, the color was probably introduced at the 1931 Pittsburgh trade show. A February 1931 trade journal article had this to say: "New Colors for Cambridge. As its new colors in glassware, the Cambridge Glass Co. offered 'Carmen,' a bright ruby and 'Burgundy,' a deep amethyst...." Cambridge Amethyst is a rich color and, although quite deep in tone, is typical of the softness of appearance that exemplifies the darker Cambridge colors.

An August 1931 trade journal had this comment: "The Apple Blossom decoration in silver on Amethyst makes up one of the most delightful of all the new Cambridge items. This is offered in a wide selection of table pieces."

Not quite four years later, an illustration of a Doulton pitcher and tumblers appeared in *China, Glass and Lamps* with a caption that read: "The out of the ordinary beverage set shown at right center has just been introduced to the market by the Cambridge Glass Co. This jug is a reproduction of an old Doulton piece. The set illustrated is in jade green, a new treatment combining matt and bright effect, and it is also made in almond, icicle and grape in the same combination of matt and bright effect." The treatment consisted of acid etching the interior (matt) of the pieces while leaving the exterior natural (bright). The parent color for Grape was, of course, Amethyst.

Amethyst was one of the few colors that was never discontinued by the original Cambridge Glass Co. and was also produced by the reorganized company during its years of operation.

Row 1
1) #3400/38, 80 ounce ball jug, etched Apple Blossom, silver encrusted. $600.00.
2) #3126, 10 ounce goblet, Crystal stem and foot. $40.00.
3) #1234, 10" footed vase, Crystal stem and foot. $75.00.
4) #3400/46, 12 ounce flask decanter. $150.00.
5) #1242, 10" vase, etched Gloria, gold encrusted. $850.00.

Row 2
1) #3400/103, 6½" globe vase, D/Japonica. $2,800.00.
2) #3078, 11 ounce goblet. $25.00.
3) Caprice #246, 7½" wide vase. $175.00.
4) Caprice #178, 80 ounce jug, Farber chrome holder. $2,000.00.

Row 3
1) #3400/10, 11" handled sandwich tray. $60.00.
2, 4) #3400/92, 2½ ounce tumblers, Farber chrome holders. $15.00 each.
3) #3400/113, 35 ounce decanter, Farber chrome holder. $65.00.
5) Blown insert in Farber chrome Nude comport. $40.00.
6) #497, 16 ounce ranch tumbler, spiral optic. $20.00.

Row 4
1) #3105 Pressed Rose Point goblet, Crystal stem and foot. $75.00.
2) Tally-Ho #1402/100 low sherbet, Crystal stem and foot. $35.00.
3, 4) #627, 4" candlesticks, Charleton Rose decoration. $250.00.
5) #3400/45 11", four-toed bowl, fancy edge, etched Gloria, gold encrusted. $600.00.

Plate 27

59

ROYAL BLUE

Royal blue is a deep, almost dark, transparent blue appropriately described as royal. Cambridge began producing Royal Blue sometime during the first half of 1931. Trade journal reports, published in February 1931, describing the Pittsburgh trade show held the previous month, make no mention of it. The Cambridge advertisement in the 1931 *China, Glass and Lamps* trade directory does include Royal Blue in the list of available colors. The available copy of the advertisement is not dated but in all probability would have been issued early in the year. The first trade journal reference to Royal Blue comes in June 1931: "This same company [Cambridge] is making short dinner lines, as well as stemware, in two rich colors, royal blue and amethyst, and of course, there are pieces of flatware in each of these colors."

Used as one of the primary colors for the Tally-Ho line, Royal Blue continued as a production color until 1943 when wartime shortages forced it to be discontinued. Postwar changes in the buying habits of the American public precluded resumption of its production. The striking beauty of Royal Blue created a desirability during the 1930s and early 1940s and once again makes it popular with today's collectors.

Row 1
1) Nautilus #3450, 11½" footed vase. $100.00.
2) Tally-Ho #1402/100 goblet, Crystal stem and foot, platinum grape decoration.* $175.00.
3) #3400/9, 7" candy box and cover, D/Japonica. $3,000.00.
4) #6004, 10" footed vase, sterling silver fruit decoration.* $500.00.
5) Seashell #47, 9½" cornucopia vase, Crystal foot. $200.00.

Row 2
1) #1066, 5½" low comport, Crystal stem and foot. $45.00.
2) #3400/851 ice pail, signed. $85.00.
3, 4) #3400/77 salt and pepper shaker, Crystal foot. $60.00 pair.
5) #3400/38, 80 ounce ball jug, etched Gloria, silver encrusted. $1,250.00.
6) #3400, 12 ounce pinch stein, etched Portia. $125.00.

Row 3
1) #1330 sweet potato vase. $50.00.
2) #3400/141, 80 ounce jug, sterling silver decoration.* $850.00.
3) Mt. Vernon #1 nine ounce goblet. $40.00.
4) #3400/54 cup and saucer, signed. $30.00.
5) Tally-Ho #1402/2, 14 ounce goblet, sterling silver decoration.* $125.00.

Row 4
1) #1321, 28 ounce sherry decanter, Crystal stem and foot, sterling silver flamingo decoration.* $850.00.
2) # 3122 nine ounce footed tumbler, Crystal stem and foot. $40.00.
3) #3112 three ounce cocktail, Crystal stem. $45.00.
4) #3400/92, 32 ounce ball decanter, six #1901 two ounce tumblers, in Farber chrome holders, Farber chrome tray. $135.00 set.
5) #1307 three-lite candlestick. $75.00.

* Decoration not done by Cambridge.

Plate 28

Row 1

1) #3400/78 cocktail shaker, Crystal ground in stopper. $200.00.
2) #1066, 12" footed vase, Crystal stem and foot. $150.00.
3) Jefferson #1401, 10 ounce goblet. $45.00.
4) Martha Washington #58, 6½" ice tub. $100.00.
5) #278, 11" footed vase, Crystal foot, gold silk screen D/1037. $450.00.

Row 2

1, 2) #3500/15 individual sugar and creamer. $60.00 set.
3) #1242, 10" vase, etched Chintz, gold encrusted. $850.00.
4) #3400/38, 12 ounce tumbler, etched Portia. $75.00.
5) #1236, 7½" ivy ball, Crystal stem and foot. $80.00.
6) #3400/144 cigarette holder, Crystal stem and ashtray foot. $75.00.
7) Nautilus #3450, 84 ounce jug. $125.00.

Row 3

1) #3400/107, 76 ounce jug and cover. $200.00.
2) #3400/92, 32 ounce ball decanter. $75.00.
3) #3500/45, 10" urn vase, etched Minerva, gold encrusted. $1,250.00.
4) #3400/136, 6" four-toed bowl, fancy edge. $85.00.

Row 4

1) #3104 nine ounce goblet, Crystal stem and foot. $175.00.
2, 4) #3400/646, 5" candlesticks, etched Wildflower, gold encrusted. $600.00 pair.
3) #3400/4, 12" four-toed bowl, etched Wildflower, gold encrusted. $1,200.00.
5) #3104 seven ounce tall sherbet, Crystal stem and foot. $150.00.

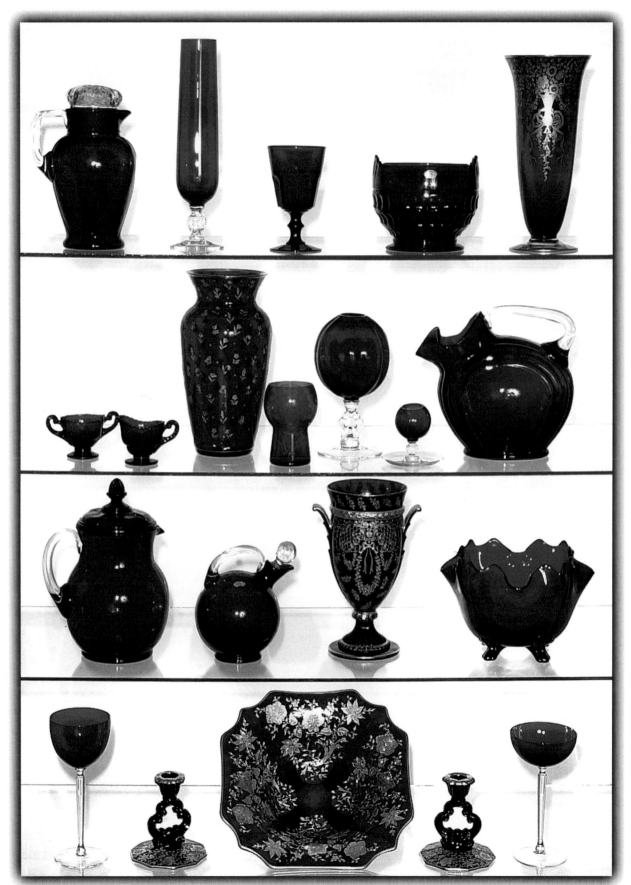

Plate 29

Introduced in August and September 1931, Forest Green is one of the colors formulated by Henry Hellmers during his stay at Cambridge. It is a dark shade of transparent green that tends toward yellow.

The first report of Forest Green in the trade journals dates to August 1931 and reads: "Cambridge Glass Co. is showing a number of very attractive new offerings for fall in its permanent showroom Room 1547, Merchandise Mart, Chicago. Among the most unusual of these items is a new color by Cambridge called Forest Green. This color is available in a wide variety of pieces."

In an April 1935 trade journal an illustration of a Doulton jug and 3400/100 tumblers appeared with this caption: "The out of the ordinary beverage set shown at right center has just been introduced to the market by Cambridge.... The jug is a reproduction of an old Doulton piece. The set illustrated is in jade green, a new treatment combining matt and bright effect, and it is also made in almond, icicle and grape in the same combination of matt and bright effect." The treatment consisted of acid etching the interior of each piece but not the exterior surfaces. The colors named were actually not new colors, just new names for pieces in Forest Green, Amber, Crystal, and Amethyst that had been so treated. Due to the relative scarcity of these sets, their production probably did not last more than one season.

Forest Green remained in the Cambridge line until 1943. Then in 1949, a new transparent dark green color, Emerald, was introduced. Beginning collectors often confuse the two greens. However, with rare exception, pieces made in Forest Green were never made in the 1949 Emerald, commonly referred to as "Late Dark Emerald." Thus, once the collector learns the time periods for the various Cambridge lines, it is easy to identify the color.

Row 1
1) #3400/38, 80 ounce ball jug, etched Bordeaux, gold encrusted. $750.00.
2) #3400/79 six ounce tall oil, Crystal foot. $125.00.
3) #3126 nine ounce goblet, Crystal bowl, Forest Green stem and foot. $125.00.
4) #3500/109, 11" four-toed ram's head bowl. $200.00.
5) #1242, 10" vase, etched Portia, gold encrusted. $750.00.

Row 2
1) Martha Washington #1400, 10 ounce goblet. $30.00.
2) #3400/46, 12 ounce flask decanter, etched Apple Blossom, brass frame. $300.00.
3) #3077, 5½ ounce cafe parfait. $25.00.
4) #3400/120, 64 ounce ball cocktail shaker, #5 chrome top, etched Diane. $400.00.
5) Tally-Ho #1402/5 seven ounce tall sherbet, gold silk screen D/1007/8. $75.00.
6) Tally-Ho #1402/39, 34 ounce decanter. $75.00.

Row 3
1) Seashell #SS17, 9" three-toed bowl, signed. $125.00.
2) Marmalade in Farber chrome holder. $30.00.
3) Everglade #17, 13" "swans" bowl, rolled edge. $125.00.
4) #3400/106 ball shaped marmalade. $60.00.
5) Rum jug. $100.00.

Row 4
1) #3400/151, 80 ounce Doulton jug. $150.00.
2) Mt. Vernon #84, 14 ounce stein, signed. $50.00.
3) Caprice #246, 7½" wide vase. $200.00.
4) #3122 three ounce cocktail, Crystal stem and foot. $35.00.
5) #158, 9" artichoke plate. $75.00.

Plate 30

Amber returned to the Cambridge catalog in 1930 and remained a staple color until the 1954 demise of the original company. Formulas were revised in the early 1930s and it is possible there is a variation in the color depth between the pre- and post-1930 Ambers but no differentiation other than by blank is made.

In the early spring of 1935, Cambridge brought out a beverage set that featured what is now called by Cambridge collectors a Doulton pitcher. Pictured in one of the trade journals, its caption read in part: "...The set illustrated is in jade green, a new treatment combining matt and bright effect, and it is also made in almond, icicle and grape in the same combination of matt and bright effect." The base color for Almond was Amber and the treatment consisted of acid etching the interior of the piece while leaving the exterior natural or non-etched.

Row 1
1) Martha Washington #18, 11" footed vase. $75.00.
2, 3) #3500/32, 6½" candelabra with Amber bobeches and Crystal prisms. $200.00 pair.
4) Mt. Vernon #13, 12 ounce tumbler in copper holder. $40.00.
5) #3400/38, 80 ounce ball jug, etched Lorna. $400.00.

Row 2
1) Tally-Ho #1402/3, 10 ounce goblet, etched Imperial Hunt Scene. $125.00.
2) Martha Washington #1400 two ounce wine. $20.00.
3) #1411, 7" rose bowl, diamond optic. $75.00.
4) #3121 three ounce cocktail, Crystal stem and foot, etch Rose Point, gold encrusted. $400.00.
5) #3104 five ounce tall hoch, Crystal bowl, Amber stem and foot. $125.00.
6, 7) Everglade #26 sugar and creamer. $75.00 set.

Row 3
1) #935, 64 ounce jug, etched #720, gold encrusted. $300.00.
2) #611 eight ounce stein. $40.00.
3) #1312, 3½" cigarette box and cover, Crystal stem and foot. $85.00.
4) Caprice #1, 10 ounce goblet. $200.00.
5) #617 cigarette jar and cover, etched #731. $75.00.
6) Tally-Ho #1402/50, 74 ounce tankard jug. $75.00.

Row 4
1, 3) #1272, 10½" candelabra, Crystal bobeches and prisms, bobeche and foot etched Apple Blossom. $300.00 pair.
2) #3400/4, 12" four-toed bowl, etched Minerva, gold encrusted. $200.00.
4) #1369, 36 ounce melon fluted decanter. $75.00.

A new Cambridge catalog was issued in 1930 with supplemental pages following during the next four years. The 1931 supplement contained a page that featured silver decorated Ebony ware. From then until October 1943, when it was discontinued, Ebony remained in the Cambridge line although perhaps not in continuous production. It was in the 1930s and 1940s that etched, silver, white gold, and yellow gold encrusted pieces were produced, as were those with transfer enamel decorations.

Ebony returned to the Cambridge catalog in September 1950 and it remained in the line until October 1953. Price lists issued by the reorganized company during the years 1955 – 1958 made no mention of Ebony, indicating the color was not made during that time period.

Since the color itself does not indicate a production date, other factors indicate when a specific piece was made: the shape of the piece; if decorated, the type of decoration as well as the actual decoration; or if etched, the etching.

Row 1
1) #1621, 10" footed urn vase, D/450. $125.00.
2) #3085, 10 ounce footed tumbler, etched Imperial Hunt Scene, gold encrusted. $600.00.
3) #430, 12" bowl, etched Rose Point, gold encrusted. $1,200.00.
4) #882 tobacco humidor and cover, with inner moistener lid, etched Golf Scene, gold encrusted. $1,200.00.
5) #277, 9" footed vase, etched Chantilly, gold encrusted. $600.00.

Row 2
1) #391, 8" ashtray, D/450. $25.00.
2) #3400/69 A. D. cup and saucer, signed. $45.00.
3) #3400/45, 11" four-toed bowl, fancy edge, etched Blossom Time, gold encrusted, exterior gold trim. $450.00.
4) #1352 frog vase. $400.00.
5) #300, 7" three-footed candy box and cover, etched Wildflower, gold encrusted. $800.00.

Row 3
1, 2, 4, 5) #3400/92, 2½ ounce tumblers. $10.00 each.
3) #3400/92, 32 ounce ball decanter. $60.00.
6) Martha #453, 11" low footed bowl, flared. $100.00.
7) #1191, 6" "Cherub" candlestick. $400.00.
8) Nautilus #3450, 11" footed vase. $75.00.
9 Statuesque #3011/9 three ounce cocktail, Crystal bowl, Ebony stem and foot. $125.00.

Row 4
1) #118, 7" wide basket, sterling silver floral decoration.* $700.00.
2) #617 cigarette jar and lid, sterling silver floral decoration.* $300.00.
3) #1070, 36 ounce pinch decanter, sterling silver Scotch decoration.* $100.00.
4) #3120 three ounce cocktail, Aero Optic, Crystal bowl, Ebony stem and foot, silver trim rim and foot. $45.00.
5) #3400/38, 80 ounce ball jug, etched Gloria, silver encrusted. $750.00.
6) #3400/17, 12" vase, sterling silver floral decoration, signed Rockwell.* $500.00.

*Decoration not done by Cambridge.

Plate 32

69

Heatherbloom is what is known as a changeable color and as such can be deceiving. When viewed in natural light (daylight) or under incandescent artificial light, it is a delicate pale orchid or lavender. When viewed under fluorescent light, it generally takes on a light blue or gray appearance. This light-dependent variation in color is due to the presence of neodymium in the formula.

The first known mention of Heatherbloom in the trade journals occurred in November 1931. It probably first appeared in the Cambridge showrooms some time in September or early October. This would have given the trade journal reporters time to visit the showroom, write the article and meet deadlines for a November issue. One comment in the article was: "...and the delicate new Heatherbloom." Later this same article went on to say: "Speaking of heatherbloom, the factory has a short line of dinnerware, stemware and a few odd pieces in this new color which is so exactly the shade of the heatherbell. And it may be had either plain or decorated with the Apple Blossom or the Gloria etchings."

When viewing a large collection of Heatherbloom, it is readily apparent there are two distinct shades of the color. The original color was developed by Henry Hellmers and before he left Cambridge, he revised the formula, hence the two shades.

This color could be confused with crystal which has taken on a lavender shade by prolonged exposure to sunlight. However, the fact that Heatherbloom is a changeable color helps in distinguishing sun-colored glass since it does not change hue under fluorescent light.

At some point it appears attempts were made to create a color like Heatherbloom that did not use neodymium and hence was not light variable. Signed Cambridge pieces resembling Heatherbloom in color (under natural light) but do not change under fluorescent lighting are known.

The last trade journal reference to Heatherbloom occurred in 1935, indicating the color was probably not offered after that year.

Row 1
1, 3) Mt. Vernon #38, 13½" candelabra, Crystal bobeches and prisms. $1,500.00 pair.
2) Statuesque #3011/2 table goblet, etched Apple Blossom. $2,000.00.

Row 2
1) Martha Washington #56, 12 ounce stein. $85.00.
2) #3035 six ounce tall sherbet, Crystal stem and foot, etched #731. $75.00.
3) #3400/94, 3½" ball puff box. $200.00.
4) Martha Washington #1400, 10 ounce goblet. $85.00.
5) #3400/91, 8" three-handled relish, etched Gloria. $175.00.
6) Georgian #317 five ounce tumbler. $45.00.
7 #3400/38, 80 ounce ball jug, etched Portia. $750.00.

Row 3
1) Mt. Vernon #33, 4½" wide comport, Crystal stem and foot. $150.00.
2) Mt. Vernon #29, 2½ ounce mustard. $125.00.
3) Mt. Vernon #9, 8" urn and cover, footed. $150.00.
4) Georgian #316 sundae. $40.00.
5) #3122, 12 ounce footed ice tea, Crystal stem and foot. $60.00.
6) #1311, 4" footed ashtray, Crystal stem and foot. $150.00.
7) #3126 three ounce cocktail, Crystal stem and foot, etched Portia. $85.00.
8) #3400/37 salt shaker. $100.00.

Row 4
1) #3121, 10 ounce goblet, Heatherbloom bowl, stem and foot. $200.00.
2) #1312, 3½" cigarette box and cover, Crystal stem and foot, etched Portia. $350.00.
3) #1066, 11 ounce goblet, Crystal stem and foot, etched Gloria. $125.00.
4, 5) Decagon #647, 6" two-lite candlesticks. $200.00 pair.

Plate 33

"The Chicago showrooms of the Cambridge Glass Co. are displaying the 'Crown Tuscan' line which has been received with much interest since its recent announcement. This opaque glass with its rich cream-like color is offered in a wide choice of fancy and table pieces including vases, bowls, side-dishes, ball jugs, etc. This Cambridge line carries a hall-mark on the bottom of each piece after the manner of dinnerware. This hall-mark consists of a crown with the name 'Tuscan.'" The preceding came from the September 1932 issue of *China, Glass and Lamps*. The Crown Tuscan signature or hall-mark is reproduced on page 74.

Crown Tuscan is a pinkish color, sometimes described as being "near flesh color," that ranges from opaque to near translucent in density, the former being the most prevalent. It is found in a wide range of shades, from a dark tan through shades of pink to almost white. One contemporary writer, a few months after its introduction, described it as "a whitish pink opaque glass." As was the case for a number of the Cambridge colors, there were two Crown Tuscan formulas; one used for blown ware and one used when pressed ware was being made. This could account for some of the shade variations seen in the finished product.

Crown Tuscan will frequently be found with a class of hand-painted decorations known as "Charleton." "Charleton" was a registered trademark owned by Abels, Wasserberg and Co., Inc., New York City, New York. The company bought blanks from Cambridge, as well as other companies, and applied the decorations in their factory.

The similarity between Crown Tuscan and the Aladdin Lamp Company's Alacite often raises the question "did Cambridge make the lamp bases for Aladdin?" The answer is "no." The two colors were developed by the same individual, Henry Hellmers, with Crown Tuscan preceding Alacite by ten years.

Crown Tuscan proved to be a popular color and remained in the Cambridge line until sometime between the spring of 1952 and the fall of 1953.

Row 1
1) #53, 8" dolphin epergne, Crown Tuscan candlestick base and vases, Crystal arm. $750.00.
2) Nautilus #3450, 2½ ounce tumbler. $125.00.
3) #3500/42, 12" urn lamp, gold Rose Point advertising. $750.00.
4) #3500/39, 11" footed cake plate, Crown Tuscan signature, etched Portia, gold encrusted. $350.00.

Row 2
1) #1043, 8½" swan, Style III, gold trim. $175.00.
2) Nautilus #3450 salt shaker. $125.00.
3) #1228, 9" pillow vase, Crown Tuscan signature, etched Gloria, gold encrusted. $1,500.00.
4) Statuesque #3011, 9" candlestick, etched Candlelight, gold encrusted. $600.00.

Row 3
1) #1309, 5" vase, etched Rose Point, gold encrusted. $150.00.
2) Mt. Vernon #102 individual oval salt, signed, gold trim. $35.00.
3) Pristine #P384, 11" oval bowl. $75.00.
4) Pristine #P575, 9" cornucopia vase. $75.00.

Row 4
1) Seashell #SS16, 7" comport, Rockwell sterling silver seahorse decoration.* $300.00.
2) Seashell #SS47, 9½" cornucopia vase, Rockwell sterling silver seahorse decoration.* $650.00.
3) #3500/69, 6½" three-compartment relish. $65.00.
4) #647, 6" two-lite candlestick, etched Gloria, gold encrusted. $300.00.

*Decoration not done by Cambridge.

Plate 34

Seen here is the Crown Tuscan signature used by Cambridge during the color's early production years. Done in black on the bottom of the piece, it is shown here considerably larger than its actual size.

Row 1
1) #1305, 10" globe vase, footed $125.00.
2) Seashell SS#40, 10" flower or fruit center, Charleton Gardenia decoration. $450.00.
3) #3500/1 cup and saucer. $125.00.
4) #3500/5, 8½" salad plate. $50.00.

Row 2
1) #1066 oval cigarette holder with ashtray foot, Crown Tuscan signature, etched Diane, gold encrusted. $600.00.
2) #1228, 9" pillow vase, Crown Tuscan signature, gold silk screen D/1007/8. $600.00.
3) Everglade #29, 6" vase. $300.00.
4) #1301, 10" footed vase, etched Candlelight, gold encrusted. $200.00.
5) #1236, 7½" ivy ball. $75.00.

Row 3
1) #3400/114, 64 ounce ball jug, etched Chintz, gold encrusted. $1,200.00.
2) #3500/57, 8" three-part candy box and cover, etched Wildflower, gold encrusted. $400.00.
3) #1119 eagle bookend. $750.00.
4) #1506/1, 4" novelty basket, signed. $60.00.

Row 4
1) Seashell #SS11, 7" wide Nude comport, Charleton Blue Mist decoration. $450.00.
2) #6004, 6" footed vase, Ebony foot. $150.00.
3) Seashell #SS10, 5" wide comport, Charleton Roses decoration. $175.00.
4) #1237, 9" footed vase, gold trim. $75.00.

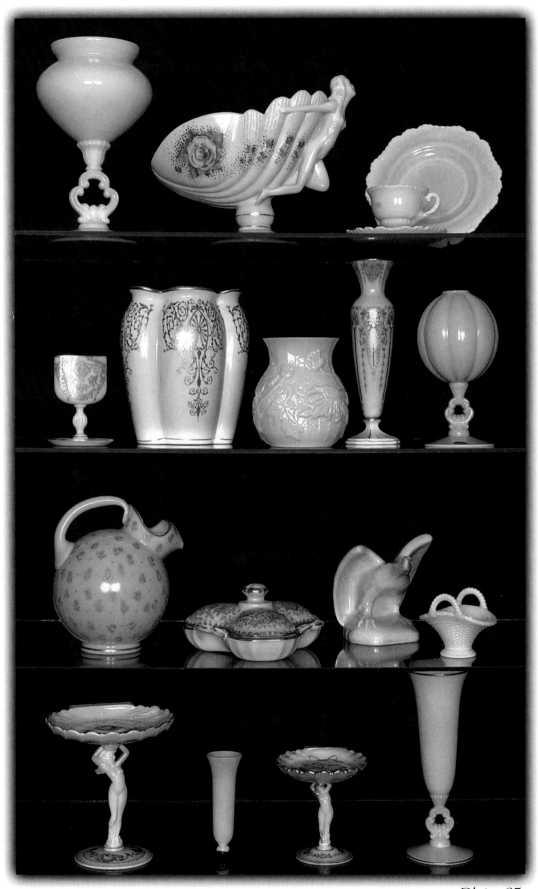

Plate 35

Cambridge introduced Rose Point at the 1935 Pittsburgh trade show and at the same show exhibited the Sea Shell line for the first time. "Sea Shell is a new Cambridge Glass Co. creation... marine motifs with the shell predominating... produced in new, translucent coral color and also in carmen, amber, royal blue, forest green and amethyst." Thus began a February 1935 trade journal article describing what was new at Cambridge for 1935.

The March 1935 issue of *China, Glass and Lamps* had a full page Cambridge advertisement for the Sea Shell line, the text of which read: "As refreshing as a May breeze is this new and delightful 'Sea Shell' line decorated with the modeled figure of a sea maid. Embracing such items as compotes, candlesticks, centerpieces, sea-food cocktails, bowls, plates, vases and relishes, its colors of Amber, Carmen, Royal Blue, Coral, Amethyst and Forest Green present a variety of the widest range. Shells, dolphins and sea maid motifs have inspired these shapes. You will be delighted to sell them."

"...The seafood cocktail and salad plate are shown in the new Coral color, a new glass shade with a tinting of Coral on bluish white. The Sea Shell line also is made in amber, carmen, royal blue, amethyst, green, and crystal." So wrote an unknown columnist in April 1935.

Because of these trade reports and Cambridge advertising, there has been much debate whether or not Coral was a distinct color, separate from Crown Tuscan. No substantial evidence has been found that there was a separate formula for Coral. The name Coral was used only in conjunction with the Sea Shell line; no other lines were ever listed as being available in Coral. By 1945 the name Coral disappeared from Cambridge price lists and what remained of the Sea Shell line was available in Crystal and Crown Tuscan. The generally accepted theory is that Coral was a color name created by the Cambridge sales department and not a formulated color.

Row 1
1) Seashell #SS51, 8" dolphin candelabrum, Crystal bobeche and prisms. $150.00.
2) Seashell #SS11, 7" wide Nude comport, signed. $150.00.
3) Seashell #SS47, 9½" cornucopia vase. $75.00.

Row 2
1) Seashell #SS46, 7½" shell flower holder, Charleton Roses decoration with gold trim. $125.00.
2) Seashell #SS21, 6" footed candy box and cover, gold trim. $85.00.
3) Seashell #SS46, 6" flower center, Charleton Rose decoration. $125.00.

Row 3
1) Seashell #SS16, 7" comport, Charleton Gardenia decoration. $75.00.
2) Seashell #SS1, 5" bread and butter plate, Charleton Roses decoration. $40.00.
3) Seashell 9" plate. $85.00.
4) Seashell #SS33, 4" three-toed ashtray, gold trim. $15.00.
5) Seashell #SS2, 7" salad plate, Rockwell sterling seahorse decoration*. $200.00.

Row 4
1) Seashell #SS30, 9" four-toed, three-compartment relished, signed. $65.00.
2) Seashell #SS48, 9" belled vase. $50.00.
3) Seashell #SS17, 9" three-toed bowl, signed. $75.00.

*Decoration not done by Cambridge.

Plate 36

Moonlight is a light, transparent blue that is slightly deeper in color than Willow Blue. Moonlight tends to collect in the heavier portions of the glass and this causes the color to appear darker or lighter depending upon the thickness of the blank being viewed.

Moonlight was introduced concurrently with Caprice and that line saw the most extensive use of the color. It was used in conjunction with the Everglade and Gyro Optic lines and also saw limited usage in other lines. Moonlight continued in the Cambridge line throughout the 1940s and into the 1950s. Moonlight Caprice was offered in the March 1952 price list but was omitted from the October 1953 edition marking the end of its production.

Numerous collectors tend to call this color Moonlight Blue. However, the correct Cambridge name for the color, as produced by the original company, is Moonlight, omitting the word blue. The second company did name its production of the same color Moonlight Blue.

Row 1
1) Nine ounce goblet. $45.00.
2) Caprice #300 nine ounce goblet. $40.00.
3) Caprice #10, 10 ounce footed tumbler. $40.00.
4) Caprice #124, 8½" three-part celery and relish. $40.00.
5, 6) Caprice #70, 7" candlesticks with prism. $85.00 pair.

Row 2
1) #497, 16 ounce ranch tumbler, spiral optic. $20.00.
2) Modern 10½" bowl. $50.00.
3) "Stackaway" five-piece ashtray set, chrome holder. $40.00 set.
4) #3500/64, 12" three-part celery and relish. $75.00.
5) Jefferson #1401, 10 ounce goblet. $50.00.

Row 3
1) Caprice #300 three ounce cocktail, Alpine finish. $50.00.
2) Caprice #201 ice bucket, four footed, Alpine finish. $175.00.
3) #647, 6" two-lite candlestick, Alpine finish. $60.00.
4) Caprice #183, 80 ounce jug. $275.00.
5) Caprice 5" ball vase. $100.00.

Row 4
1) Caprice #66, 13" four-footed crimped bowl. $75.00.
2) #1956/1, 10" ashtray, called "hambone ashtray" by collectors. $40.00.
3) Cascade #573, 9½" vase. $250.00.
4) Corinth #3900, 13" cake salver. $150.00.

Plate 37

Apparently introduced in mid-year 1937, the opaque color Windsor Blue is a lighter shade than Azurite. In its only trade journal reference, Windsor Blue was described as "a tone of icy blue in opaque glass, appearing in a small group of decorative items in the Shell shape...." Since Edward VIII, the British King, had abdicated his throne and became Duke of Windsor in 1936, at least one Cambridge authority believes the color was named Windsor Blue in his honor.

While used almost exclusively for the Shell line, there are two notable exceptions, a Tally-Ho line cocktail shaker and the two-lite 3400/647 or key hole candelabrum. The latter, while shown with the Shell line, is technically not a part of the line since it was introduced much earlier and was also shown with other lines.

John Degenhart also used Windsor Blue in some of his private mold work. His slipper with kitten, slipper with bow, and Daisy and Button hat are all known in Windsor Blue. John Degenhart was an employee of the Cambridge Glass Co. for almost 40 years. Prior to opening his own factory in 1947, he had an arrangement with the Cambridge Glass Co. to produce his own items using Cambridge glass in his private molds and working on his own time.

Windsor Blue was out of production by January 1, 1940. Precisely how long it remained in the Cambridge line is not clear. The name Windsor Blue did appear in the list of Cambridge colors published in the 1939 Cambridge pocket diary. However, Mocha, Pistachio, and La Rosa did not, which raises questions about the accuracy of the listing.

Row 1
1, 3) Statuesque #3011, 9" candlesticks with Crystal bobeches and prisms. $1,800.00.
2) Seashell SS#40, 10" flower or fruit center (often referred to by collectors as "Flying Lady Bowl"). $3,000.00.

Row 2
1) Seashell #SS11, 7" wide Nude comport, signed. $500.00.
2) Seashell #SS31, 8" oval dish, four footed. $125.00.
3) Seashell #SS47, 9½" cornucopia vase. $250.00.

Row 3
1) Seashell #SS44, 6" flower center. $225.00.
2) Seashell #SS36 cigarette box and cover, four toed, 4½" x 3½". $150.00.
3) Daisy and Button cat shoe, made for John Degenhart. $100.00.
4) Seashell #SS21, 6" footed candy box and cover. $175.00.

Row 4
1) Seashell #SS18, 10" three-toed bowl, signed. $250.00.
2) Seashell #SS213, 2½" three-toed ashtray. $45.00.
3) Seashell #SS#14, 9" comport, signed. $200.00.

Plate 38

La Rosa is a medium to light pink color that shows gathering tendencies. In the thicker areas of an item the color is very strong, while in the thinner areas the color is weak and transparent.

By March 1938, La Rosa Caprice was being advertised in consumer magazines such as *Ladies' Home Journal*. It was probably first shown to the trade at the January 1938 Pittsburgh trade show.

The primary usage of La Rosa was in the Gyro Optic line and in the Caprice line, with over 150 pieces of La Rosa Caprice available, according to Cambridge advertising. In addition, La Rosa was one of the colors utilized in "Varitone sets."

Production of La Rosa, along with that of numerous other colors, ceased in October 1943.

Pistachio was probably first shown to the trade in January 1938 at the Pittsburgh trade show. A trade journal article, published in February 1938, referenced the then new Gyro Optic line: "Also new — the Gyro-Optic design, a swirl optic and twisted rope stem done in stemware, beverage sets and flower holders in such shades as moonlight, mocha, pistachio and crystal...." Pistachio is the lightest of all the Cambridge transparent green colors. It has more of a gathering effect than Light Emerald and will appear to have more color in the thicker areas of a blank than apparent in the thinner areas or in blown ware. Once both Light Emerald and Pistachio have been seen, the collector will have no difficulty in distinguishing between the two colors. Pistachio was discontinued during October 1943.

The name Pistachio was later used by the second company but for an entirely different shade.

Row 1 La Rosa
1) Caprice #183, 80 ounce ball jug. $850.00.
2) Stradivari #3575, 3½ ounce cocktail, Crystal stem and foot. $30.00.
3) Caprice #32, 11" four-footed cabaret plate. $75.00.
4) Caprice #300, 12 ounce footed tumbler, Crystal foot. $50.00.
5) Caprice #300 nine ounce goblet, Crystal stem and foot. $60.00.
6) #3187 cocktail. $20.00.

Row 2 La Rosa
1) Stradivari #3575, one ounce cordial, Crystal stem and foot. $50.00.
2) Statuesque #3011/9 three ounce cocktail, Crystal stem and foot. $175.00.
3) #1327 one ounce cordial or favor vase. $25.00.
4) Caprice #65, 11" four-footed handled oval bowl, Alpine finish. $125.00.
5) Caprice # 235, 6" four-footed rose bowl. $250.00.
6) Caprice #152, 6" two-handled lemon plate. $40.00.
7) Georgian #319, 12 ounce tumbler. $25.00.

Row 3 Pistachio
1) Georgian #319, 12 ounce tumbler. $25.00.
2) Georgian #319/B/2 basket, Crystal handle. $60.00.
3) Stradivari #3575 one ounce cordial, Crystal stem and foot. $50.00.
4) Caprice #300 one ounce cordial, Crystal stem and foot. $200.00.
5, 6) Martha #250 individual sugar and creamer. $40.00 set.
7) Georgian #319 nine ounce tumbler. $20.00.
8) Georgian #317S sherbet. $20.00.

Row 4 Pistachio
1) Gyro Optic #3143, 10 ounce goblet, Crystal stem and foot. $65.00.
2, 3) Caprice #38 sugar and creamer, medium size. $75.00 set.
4) Caprice #214, 3" ashtray. $25.00.
5) Caprice #17 cup. $35.00.
6) Statuesque #3011/9 three ounce cocktail, Crystal stem and foot. $175.00.
7) Statuesque #3011 three ounce cocktail, middle size nude, Crystal stem and foot. $275.00.
8) Statuesque #3011/2 table goblet, Crystal stem and foot. $400.00.

Plate 39

Mocha is a soft shade of amber that is lighter than the Amber of the same time period. Thicker areas of a blank appear darker in color due to a bunching effect.

Mocha was probably shown to the trade for the first time in January 1938 at the Pittsburgh trade show. A trade journal article, published in February 1938, referenced the new Gyro-Optic line: "Also new — the 'Gyro-Optic' design, a swirl optic and twisted rope stem done in stemware, beverage sets and flower holders in such shades as moonlight, mocha, pistachio and crystal...."

In addition to the Gyro Optic line, the other main uses for Mocha were the Caprice line and the Harlequin and Varitone Sets. Madeira is very similar to Mocha; however, the two colors were never used for the same line nor was Madeira used for Varitone or Harlequin Sets. If there is a question about the color, the piece is the identifier.

Mocha was among numerous colors discontinued October 1943.

Tahoe Blue, a color very similar, if not identical to Blue Bell, first appeared in the early 1940s as one of the eight colors used to create Harlequin Sets. Tahoe Blue may have been a name created by the Cambridge sales department to enhance the sales of Harlequin Sets as the name appears nowhere else in Cambridge catalogs. The color, regardless of its name, was produced again during the last years of the original company and again by the second company. It is not clear if any of the glass produced during these runs was sold commercially.

Row 1

1) Statuesque #3011/9 three ounce cocktail, Crystal stem and foot. $250.00.
2) Stradivari #3575, 3½ ounce cocktail, Crystal stem and foot. $30.00.
3) Today A56 goblet, Crystal bowl. $40.00.
4) Today A56 wine, Crystal bowl. $40.00.
5) #497, 10 ounce tumbler. $20.00.
6) #321 seven ounce old fashioned cocktail, shammed. $25.00.
7) #3700 six ounce tall sherbet, Crystal stem and foot. $75.00.
8) #1327 one ounce cordial or favor vase. $30.00.

Row 2 Tahoe Blue

1, 3) #1715 ashtrays. $20.00 each.
2) Cascade #4000/1 goblet. $200.00.
4) Pristine #P510, 2¾" ball candlestick. $75.00.
5) Experimental "overlay" or "cased" 9" vase.*
6) Caprice #216, 5" ashtray. $45.00.
7) #1371 Bridge Hound (pencil dog). $75.00.
8) Seashell #SS18, 10" three-toed bowl. $500.00.

Row 3 Mocha

1) Statuesque 3011/9 three ounce cocktail, Crystal stem and foot. $150.00.
2) #1236, 7½" ivy ball, Crystal stem and foot. $65.00.
3) #1066 seven ounce tall sherbet. $15.00.
4) Stradivari #3575, 3½ ounce cocktail, Crystal stem and foot. $25.00.
5) #1040, 3" swan, Style II, signed. $75.00.
6) Gyro Optic #3143/50, 13 ounce tumbler. $15.00.
7) #1341 one ounce cordial. $5.00.
8) #1327 one ounce cordial or favor vase. $25.00.
9) #1371 Bridge Hound (pencil dog). $25.00.

Row 4 Mocha

1) Seashell #SS34, 3" three-toed ashtray. $8.00.
2) Georgian #317, 5 ounce tumbler. $10.00.
3, 4) Caprice #38 sugar and creamer, medium size. $60.00 set.
5) Caprice #216, 5" ashtray. $50.00.
6) Caprice #22, 8½" salad plate. $20.00.
7) Caprice #17 cup and saucer. $30.00 set.

Plate 40

    Harlequin Sets were added to the Cambridge line in 1941 and in June 1941 a supplemental catalog page showing the sets was distributed. None of the items in the sets were new; rather what was unique about the sets was that each consisted of a single item in eight different colors. A January 1, 1942, letter to the Cambridge sales agents listed the eight colors as La Rosa, Moonlight, Mocha, Pistachio, Gold Krystol, Amethyst, Forest Green, and Tahoe Blue. Fourteen different Harlequin Sets were originally offered, made up of Regency cocktail; Regency cordial; 3187 cocktail; 3011 cordial; 3011 cocktail; 8, 10, and 12 ounce 3135 tumbler; 1327 cordial; 496 12 ounce Tall Joe; 10 and 12 ounce shammed 497 tumbler; 321 seven ounce old-fashioned glass, and the 319 nine ounce Georgian tumbler. Some of these same items may be found in other colors as well but whether or not such pieces were part of a Harlequin Set has not been definitively determined. Harlequin Sets were effectively discontinued in October 1943 when production of many Cambridge colors ceased due to wartime shortages.

    Late Mulberry is a name assigned by collectors to a purple color that differs from the Mulberry of the 1920s and the Amethyst of the 1930s and early 1940s. It was used to produce several items in the Caprice line, 1066 stemware, and other blanks as well. Its reason for existence is somewhat of a mystery since Amethyst was never discontinued. Production dates are somewhat illusive; indications are it was made during the 1940s and again in the 1950s.

Row 1 (back)

1 – 3) Mt. Vernon #84, 14 ounce stein, Crystal handle, signed, Royal Blue, Carmen, Amber. $50.00 – 75.00 each.
4 – 6) #3400/107, 14 ounce stein, Crystal handle: Forest Green, Royal Blue, Amber. $40.00 – 50.00 each.

Row 1 (front)

7 – 9) Mt. Vernon #84, 14 ounce stein, Crystal handle, signed: Forest Green, Gold Krystol, Heatherbloom. $50.00 – 75.00 each.
10 – 12) #3400/107, 14 ounce stein, Crystal handle: Crystal, Carmen, Gold Krystol. $40.00 – 50.00 each.

Row 2

1 – 6) #1327 cordial or favor vase, Tahoe Blue, Mocha, Forest Green, La Rosa, Pistachio, Moonlight. $25.00 – 30.00 each.
7 – 12) #3187 cocktail, Tahoe Blue, Amethyst, Mocha, Moonlight, Forest Green, Pistachio. $20.00 each.
13 – 20) Stradivari #3575 one ounce cordial, colored bowl, Crystal stem and foot, Tahoe Blue, Pistachio, Forest Green, Moonlight, Gold Krystol, La Rosa, Mocha, Amethyst. $50.00 – 60.00 each.

Row 3

1 – 6) #497, 10 ounce tumbler shammed, Forest Green, Amethyst, Tahoe Blue, Gold Krystol, Pistachio, La Rosa. $20.00 each.
7 – 10) (back row) Georgian #319 nine ounce tumbler, Forest Green, Carmen, Moonlight, La Rosa. $15.00 – 20.00 each.
11 – 14) (front row) Georgian #319 nine ounce tumbler, Amber, Gold Krystol, Amethyst, Pistachio. $15.00 – 20.00 each.

Row 4 Late Mulberry

1 – 3) #3400/92, 2½ ounce tumbler. $8.00 each.
4) #3400/92, 32 ounce ball decanter, Crystal stopper. $40.00.
5 – 7) #3400/92, 2½ ounce tumbler. $8.00 each.
8) #1066 three ounce cocktail, pale gold stem and foot. $50.00.
9) #1066 one ounce cordial, pale gold stem and foot. $100.00.
10) Caprice #301 goblet, pale gold stem and foot. $200.00.
11) Caprice #301 sherbet, pale gold stem and foot. $150.00.
12) Caprice #42, 9" oval tray. $100.00.
13, 14) Caprice #38 sugar and creamer, medium size. $125.00 set.

Plate 41

Mandarin Gold is a medium shade of yellow with considerable bunching in the heavy areas of a piece. It was a replacement for Gold Krystol, a lighter shade of yellow.

Mandarin Gold, along with Emerald, were the first new Cambridge colors in some 12 years when they were brought out during the summer of 1949. A July 1949 trade journal article references two new colors that are to be shown while another trade journal the following month makes note of two new colors being shown at the Chicago showroom. In all probability, the two colors were first seen by the trade at the 1949 summer New York trade show.

Along with Emerald, Mandarin Gold was retained in the Cambridge line throughout the last years of the original company and was also included in the reorganized company's line.

Row 1
1) #1237, 9" footed vase. $50.00.
2, 3) Pristine #P499 calla lily candlesticks. $85.00 pair.
4) Seashell #SS11, 7" wide Nude comport. $450.00.
5) Heirloom #5000/2 six ounce sherbet. $15.00.
6) Statuesque #3011/9 three ounce cocktail, Crown Tuscan stem and foot. $150.00.

Row 2
1) Georgian #319, 12 ounce tumbler. $20.00.
2) #1043, 8½" swan, Style III. $125.00.
3) #1042, 6½" swan, Style III. $100.00.
4) Seashell #SS 31, 8" oval dish, four-footed. $35.00.
5) Martha #250 individual sugar. $15.00.

Row 3
1, 2) Cascade #41 creamer and sugar. $35.00 set.
3) Statuesque #3011/3 saucer champagne, Crystal stem and foot. $250.00.
4) Statuesque #3011 ashtray, Crystal stem and foot. $300.00.
5, 6) Caprice #1338, 6" three-lite candlesticks. $125.00 pair.

Row 4
1) Caprice #214, 3" ashtray. $10.00.
2) Jefferson #1401, 10 ounce goblet. $15.00.
3) Jefferson #1401 three ounce cocktail. $15.00.
4) Jefferson #1401, 12 ounce footed tumbler. $15.00.
5) #1066, 3½ ounce cocktail. $15.00.
6) #1066 seven ounce tall sherbet. $15.00.
7) #1066 five ounce footed tumbler. $15.00.
8, 9) #1715 ashtray/candlesticks. $16.00 pair.

Plate 42

Emerald is a dark green and since the name was used twice before, today's Cambridge collectors generally call this color Late Dark Emerald. Emerald is often confused with Forest Green, a dark green of earlier production. However, these two colors were never produced concurrently and the piece will determine the color.

Emerald, along with Mandarin Gold were the first new Cambridge colors in some 12 years when they were brought out in the summer of 1949. A July 1949 trade journal references two new colors that "will be shown" while another trade journal the following month makes note of two new colors being shown at the Cambridge showroom in Chicago's Merchandise Mart. In all probability, the two colors were first seen by the trade at the 1949 summer New York trade show.

After its 1949 introduction, Emerald remained in the original company's line until it ceased operations during the summer of 1954. The reorganized or second company resumed its production and pieces in Emerald were offered in its final price list, dated 1958.

Row 1
1) Cascade #573, 9½" vase. $75.00.
2) Caprice #133, 6" low footed bonbon, square. $40.00.
3) Seashell #SS11, 7" wide Nude comport. $450.00.
4) #1066, 12 ounce footed ice tea, Crystal stem and foot. $20.00.
5) #3900/575, 10" cornucopia vase. $50.00.

Row 2
1, 2) Caprice #1338, 6" three-lite candlesticks. $125.00 pair.
3) Cambridge Arms #29 six-piece unit, Crystal arm. $300.00 set.
4, 5) Cascade #41 creamer and sugar. $35.00 set.

Row 3
1) #3400, 22 ounce jug on Farber chrome foot. $45.00.
2) Seashell #SS31, 8" oval dish, four-footed, Charleton Roses decoration. $35.00.
3) #1043, 8½" swan, Style III. $125.00.
4) #1040, 3" swan, Style III. $35.00.
5) #1042, 6½" swan, Style III. $100.00.

Row 4
1) #3500/54, 6" two-handled footed bonbon. $25.00.
2) #1066, 7" footed ivy ball. $75.00.
3) Caprice #66, 13" bowl, crimped, four footed $85.00.
4) Corinth #3900/136, 5½" comport, Charleton Roses decoration. $100.00.

Plate 43

Cambridge Milk Glass is a white opaque glass with no opalescence and is somewhat of a lifeless color. It achieves its beauty from the high shine that it provides.

It would appear that Milk Glass was introduced to the trade at the January 1954 Pittsburgh trade show since a February trade journal references it among the "new offerings at Cambridge Glass." The only known trade journal advertisements for Milk Glass appeared in the July 1954 issues of *Crockery & Glass Journal* and *China, Glass and Decorative Accessories* at about the same time the decision not to resume factory operations was made. Hence, along with Ebon, it probably had one of the shortest, if not *the* shortest, production runs of any of the original company's colors. Production was not resumed by the reorganized company.

Row 1
1) W121 Scotty bookend.*
2) W133 Cascade 9½" vase. $75.00.
3) W113 Seashell five ounce seafood cocktail. $40.00.
4) W77 Mt. Vernon covered urn. $60.00.
5) W69 Mt. Vernon one ounce cordial. $25.00.
6) W93 Everglade 12 ounce mug. $45.00.

Row 2
1) W132 Martha Washington 8½" fan vase. $35.00.
2) W100 five ounce swan punch cup. $60.00.
3) W97, 8½" swan #1043, Style III. $300.00.
4) W98, 4½" swan #1041, Style III. $85.00.
5) W131 Seashell 7½" shell vase. $75.00.

Row 3
1) W126 Everglade 5" vase. $55.00.
2 W122 Pigeon bookend.*
3) W85 Mt. Vernon 4½" puff box and cover. $50.00.
4) Caprice #73 reflector candlestick. $400.00.

Row 4
1) W65 Mt. Vernon 10 ounce goblet. $30.00.
2) W90 Caprice three ounce oil, ground stopper. $100.00.
3) Mt. Vernon 5" two-lite candlestick. $75.00.
4) W92, 3½" miniature cornucopia, gold trim. $25.00.
5) W104 Seashell 9" comport, Charleton Rose decoration. $200.00.

*Due to the uniqueness of this item, no value is provided.

Plate 44

Quoting from its promotional brochure: "Ebon is a black glass with a finish totally unlike any which has been on the market before. To describe this finish is difficult; to say it has a mat finish is incorrect, it really is a rough mat finish to which has been added a luster, a dull sheen which gives it a soft beauty."

It would appear that Ebon was introduced to the trade at the January 1954 Pittsburgh trade show since a February trade journal references it among the "new offerings at Cambridge Glass." The only known trade journal advertisement for Ebon appeared in the July 1954 issue of *Crockery & Glass Journal* at about the same time the decision not to resume factory operations was made. Hence, along with Milk Glass, it probably had one of the shortest, if not *the* shortest, production runs of any of the original company's colors. Production was not resumed by the reorganized company.

With only a few exceptions such as the 628 candlestick, the 1633 peg vase, and 1536 peg nappy from the Cambridge Arms line and the 747 cigarette box and cover, the Ebon line consisted of blanks from the Cambridge Square line.

Row 1
1) Cambridge Square #58, 15½" salad bowl, D/Birds. $150.00.
2) Cambridge Square #28, 13½" plate, D/Birds. $100.00.

Row 2
1) Cambridge Square #48, 9" oval bowl, D/Birds. $75.00.
2) Cambridge Square #69 two-lite candlestick, D/Birds. $75.00.
3) Cambridge Square #81, 10" bowl, D/Birds. $85.00.
4, 5) #628, 3½" candlesticks. $80.00 pair.

Row 3
1, 2) Cambridge Square #67 candlesticks, D/Birds. $100.00 pair.
3) Cambridge Square #47, 8" bowl, D/Birds. $75.00.
4) Cambridge Square #80, 8" bud vase, D/Birds. $75.00.
5) Cambridge Square #80, 8" bud vase. $45.00.
6) Cambridge Square #80, 8" bud vase, D/Stars. $65.00.

Row 4
1) Cambridge Square #165 candy box and cover. $50.00.
2) Cambridge Square #91, 5½" vase, D/Stars. $65.00.
3) Pristine #747 cigarette box and cover. $35.00.
4) Cambridge Square #493, 1¾" candlestick. $20.00.
5) Cambridge Square #493, 1¾" candlestick, D/Stars. $30.00.
6) Pristine #737 canoe ashtray. $25.00.
7) Cambridge Square #40 cigarette urn, D/Birds. $30.00.
8) Cambridge Square #151, 3½" ashtray. $10.00.

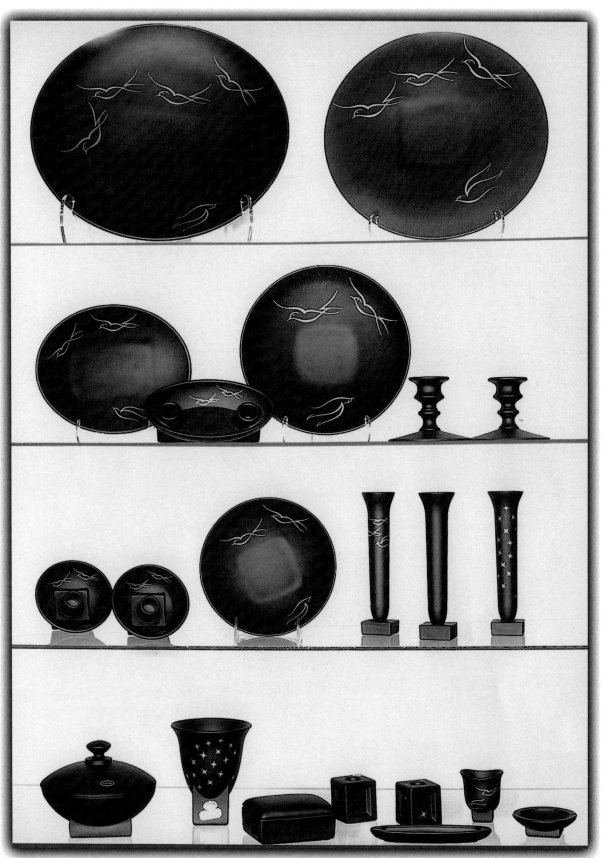

Plate 45

95

Smoke is a transparent medium gray shade that has strong suggestions of amethyst. It is a color that was developed by the reorganized or second Cambridge Glass Co. sometime between March 1955 and March 1956. It remained in the line until the company ceased operations.

Row 1
1) Sonata #1957/85 decanter. $125.00.
2) #1529 decanter, cut Starburst. $125.00.
3) Statuesque #3011, 7" comport, medium size Crystal Nude stem. $350.00.
4) Statuesque #3011/2 table goblet, Crystal stem and foot. $300.00.
5) Statuesque #3011 three ounce cocktail, middle size Crystal Nude stem. $275.00.
6) Corinth #3900/35, 13½" handled cake plate. $100.00.

Row 2
1) Heirloom #5000/22, 8" salad plate. $25.00.
2, 4) Caprice #72, 6" two-lite candlesticks. $250.00 pair.
3) #1955 three ounce tumbler. $25.00.
5) Allegro #3795 wine, bowl with crackle finish, Crystal stem and foot. $125.00.
6) Connoisseur #9, 25 ounce beer or brandy.*

Row 3
1) Statuesque #3011/9 three ounce cocktail, bowl with crackle finish, Crystal stem and foot. $600.00.
2) Statuesque #3011/3 saucer champagne, bowl with crackle finish, Crystal stem and foot. $650.00.
3) Corinth #3900/41 sugar. $45.00.
4) Corinth #3900/126, 12" three-part celery and relish. $100.00.
5) Corinth #3900/41 creamer. $45.00.
6) Georgian #317S sherbet. $20.00.
7) Corinth #3900/129 two-piece mayonnaise set. $75.00.

Row 4
1) Modern candy box and cover. $85.00.
2) Modern 11" bowl. $100.00.
3) #497, 16 ounce ranch tumbler, spiral optic. $20.00.
4) #1528, 10¼" vase. $75.00.

*Due to the uniqueness of this item, no value is provided.

Plate 46

Violet, a medium shade of opaque purple, was produced by the reorganized or second Cambridge Glass Co. It is lighter than Helio and was not used for any of the same blanks. Hence, the piece is the key to identifying Violet.

Violet colored items include blanks from the Everglade, Jenny Lind, Caprice, and Mt. Vernon lines; while Helio, a much earlier color, was used to produce items from the Plainware line and other plain shapes from the 1920s.

Violet, produced sometime between March 1955 and late 1958, must have had a very short production run since it never appeared on a published price list.

Row 1
1) Everglade #20, 10½" vase. $400.00.
2, 3) Everglade #2 candlesticks. $600.00 pair.
4) Jenny Lind #315 candy box and cover. $350.00.

Row 2
1) Mt. Vernon #2, 6½ ounce sherbet. $150.00.
2) Everglade #22, 6" vase. $300.00.
3) Seashell #SS33, 4" four-toed ashtray. $200.00.
4) Arcadia #165, 6" candy box and cover. $400.00.

Row 3
1) #1956/1, 10" ashtray, called "hambone" by collectors. $200.00.
2) Mt. Vernon #1 nine ounce goblet. $200.00.
3) Jenny Lind #321, 8" dish, crimped. $350.00.

Row 4
1) Arcadia #39, 13" oval shallow bowl, crimped. $450.00.
2) Arcadia #19, 12" oval bowl. $450.00.

Plate 47

Technically not a distinct color, the Mardi Gras line was produced using crystal (clear) glass into which was embedded flecks of glass in assorted vivid colors. The embedding process resulted in the flecks remaining intact as well as turning into swirls of color.

Mardi Gras was introduced to the trade in December 1957 by means of a trade journal advertisement and then was first seen the following month at the Pittsburgh trade show. Quoting from the advertisement: "This striking new gift line from Cambridge captures the Mardi Gras spirit in unusual contours, shapes, brilliance and gaiety! Every color of the rainbow blends to give the light, bright, touch...."

In the stemware section of the October 1956 Cambridge price list was a line called "Casual Line," with a subheading "Made in White Rain and Blue Cloud." White Rain has a crystal body with embedded flecks of a light pink opaque (possibly Crown Tuscan), while Blue Cloud has flecks of a light blue opaque. Similar but not listed on the price list are pieces with orange flecks and possibly known as "Strawberry." Also known and shown on the opposing page is a footed tumbler with brown swirls, possibly Amber and one with blue swirls different than seen in Blue Cloud. The price list only offered two pieces, the 3060 low sherbet and the 3130/2 footed tumbler. Since these are similar to Mardi Gras, today's collectors often include them in Mardi Gras collections; hence they are included here.

Row 1
1) 5A 6" pear-shaped vase. $750.00.
2) 4A 12" decanter, no stopper. $1,000.00.
3) 6A ball and neck decanter. $1,200.00.
4) 1A 12" vase. $1,000.00.

Row 2
1) Casual Line 12 ounce footed tumbler (from 3130/2 footed tumbler), brown swirls.* **
2) Casual Line 12 ounce footed tumbler (from 3130/2 footed tumbler), blue swirls.* **
3) 3B 3¼" triangle vase. $500.00.
4) 6B 3¼" x 5½" rose bowl. $600.00.
5) 2A 4½" x 5¼" rose bowl (ball vase). $650.00.

Row 3
1) 2B 5¾" shallow bowl. $600.00.
2) 7A 5¾" vase (made from #1544 water bottle mold). $750.00.
3) Small deep bowl, 4" across. $500.00.
4) 4B 5" flip vase (cylinder). $600.00.
5) Casual Line #3060 sherbet, "Strawberry."*
6) 5B 4¾" ashtray, red flecks.* **

Row 4
1) Casual Line White Rain 12 ounce footed tumbler (from 3130/2 footed tumbler). $100.00.
2) Casual Line Blue Cloud 12 ounce footed tumbler (from 3130/2 footed tumbler). $125.00.
3) 6½" shallow dish, Blue Cloud.* **
4) 5" tall triangle vase, Blue Cloud.* **
5) 6" ashtray, purple flecks.* **

*Due to the uniqueness of this item, no value is provided.

**These pieces were probably not production items.

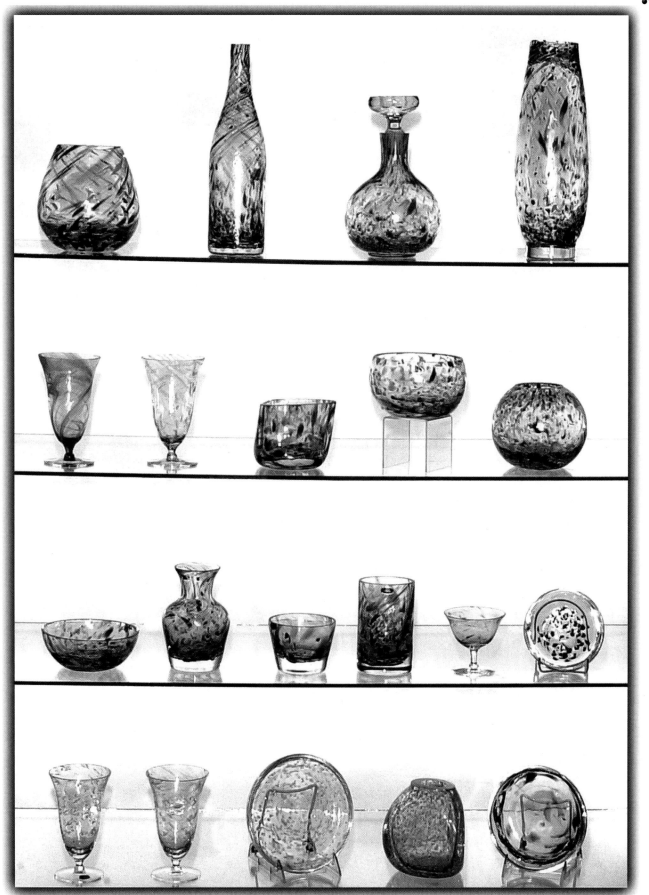

Plate 48

Amber — The original Cambridge Glass Company used the name Amber several times. The reorganized company also used it but altered the formula to produce a darker color than any of the earlier Ambers. Collectors often refer to this Amber as Late Amber to differentiate it from earlier shades.

Pink — Within the first year of its operation, the reorganized or second Cambridge Glass Co. brought out several colors. One was simply known as Pink. It is a light transparent pink color that does tend to have a slight yellow tone to it when compared to the earlier Peach-blo. However, Pink can only be unquestionably identified when the blank is one unique to the reorganized company. Pink remained in the catalog until the reorganized company ceased operations in 1959.

Pistachio is another color brought out during the first year the reorganized company operated. It is a different color than the earlier Pistachio. It is still a light transparent green, but the 1950s Pistachio is a different shade and has less sparkle. Once seen in a shape known to be unique to the reorganized company, there will be no confusion between the two colors. The 1950s Pistachio was offered in the October 1956 price list but not in the 1958 edition, the last issued.

Sunset — Similar to the 1920s Rubina, Sunset was a short-lived color produced sometime between March 1955 and mid-1958. It is a dark red at the bottom of the item shading upward through yellow and sometimes green into a light transparent blue. At the very top is a thin line of yellow and red. Sunset never appeared on a price list or in company advertising. Rubina and Sunset will not be confused since it appears the latter was used only to produce the pieces shown here.

Moonlight, Carmen, and Mandarin Gold were also produced by the reorganized company but identical to the original colors

Row 1
1) Moonlight Blue Modern candy box and cover. $65.00.
2) Moonlight Blue #1321, 28 ounce crackle sherry decanter. $350.00.
3) Moonlight Blue #497, 12 ounce crackle tumbler. $50.00.
4) Moonlight Blue #1529 decanter. $100.00.
5) Moonlight Blue controlled bubble paper weight, polished sides. $150.00.
6) Moonlight Blue #3790 goblet, cut Blue Danube. $75.00.

Row 2
1) Pistachio #1528, 10¼" vase, cut Starburst. $100.00.
2) Pistachio #1519, 10" vase. $75.00.
3) Pistachio controlled bubble paperweight. $125.00.
4) Pistachio #3011 three ounce cocktail, middle size Nude, crackle bowl, Crystal stem and foot. $600.00.
5) Pink #1955 six ounce old-fashioned tumbler. $50.00.
6) Pink #1528, 10¼" vase, cut Starburst. $100.00.
7) Pink Invitation #3791, 12 ounce footed tumbler. $25.00.
8) Pink Statuesque 3011/3 saucer champagne, crackle bowl, Crystal stem and foot. $650.00.

Row 3
1) Sunset #497, 16 ounce spiral optic ranch tumbler. $100.00.
2) Sunset #1955 three ounce tumbler. $85.00.
3) Sunset #1955, 14 ounce tumbler. $100.00.
4) Sunset #3060 sherbet. $250.00.
5) Amber Jenny Lind #318, 8¼" basket, no handle. $60.00.
6) Amber Jenny Lind creamer. $30.00.
7) Amber Jenny Lind #320 open candy. $50.00.

Row 4
1) Carmen Statuesque #3011 cocktail, middle size Nude, crackle bowl. $750.00.
2) Carmen Statuesque #3011/2 table goblet, crackle bowl. $850.00.
3) Carmen Statuesque #3011/3 saucer champagne, crackle bowl. $750.00.
4) Mandarin Gold Today #A56 goblet. $30.00.
5) Mandarin Gold controlled bubble paperweight. $125.00.
6) Mandarin Gold Statuesque #3011 three ounce cocktail, middle size Nude, crackle bowl. $600.00.
7) Mandarin Gold #1955 three ounce crackle tumbler. $50.00.

Plate 49

Over the years Cambridge tested a number of colors, colors that apparently never made it into commercial production. This plate shows a number of sample pieces in such colors. There is no evidence these colors were ever given names or sold commercially. None of the names or descriptions used here are of Cambridge origin. Due to the fact that most of these pieces are the only ones of their types known, no values are provided.

Row 1

1) Tomato #3130 seven ounce tall sherbet.
2) Orange opaque #3121, 10 ounce goblet stem, Crystal bowl.
3) Orange opaque #3400/68 creamer, signed.
4) Pale blue opaque Statuesque #3011 cupped comport, Crystal top.
5) Pale blue opaque #3400/54 cup and saucer, signed.
6) Pink opalescent Everglade #38, 10½" vase, foot leaves crimped.

Row 2

1) Pumpkin orange opaque Everglade #23, 5" vase.
2) Translucent green #3400/68 creamer, signed.
3) Custard opaque Seashell #SS1, 5" bread and butter plate.
4) Translucent green #3400/68 sugar, signed.
5) White overlay (cased) controlled bubble 7" vase, Crystal outer layer.
6) Blue opaque Seashell #SS17, 9" three-toed bowl, signed.

Row 3

1) Teal Chelsea #129, 7½" vase.
2) Rubina opaque Honeycomb 6½" comport.
3) Red slag Two Kid 8¾" figure flower holder.
4) Pink opalescent Arcadia two-handled bonbon.
5) Pink opalescent Arcadia ivy ball.
6) Blue opaque Seashell #SS1, 5" bread and butter plate.

Row 4

1) Custard opaque #390, 5¾" ashtray.
2) Amber/black translucent 9½" bowl.
3) Gold/amber opalescent #447, 6¾" comport.

Plate 50

In this, and following plates, colors are presented side by side and under identical lighting conditions so the reader may compare various colors that are often confused. Most of the opaque colors seen here date to the 1920s. The exceptions are Violet, seen on the right side of Row 3 that dates to the 1950s and Windsor Blue, Row 4, from the late 1930s.

Row 1

1) Azurite #152 marmalade and cover. $100.00.
2) Azurite #21, 3½ ounce sherbet. $75.00.
3) Azurite #20 creamer. $35.00.
4) Helio atomizer, etched #405, gold encrusted. $400.00.
5) Helio #64, 5¼" low comport. $45.00.
6) Helio #124, 3½" basket, 5" tall. $85.00.

Row 2

1) Primrose Yellow #308, 4¾" ball vase. $75.00.
2) Primrose Yellow Plymouth #2630 sherbet. $125.00.
3) Primrose Yellow ringtree. $150.00.
4) Jade perfume, gold trim. $250.00.
5) Jade #301, 6" vase. $75.00.
6) Jade #307, 3" vase, crimped. $75.00.

Row 3

1) Avocado #710 letter holder. $125.00.
2) Avocado round #933 cup and saucer. $125.00.
3) Avocado #3085, 4½ ounce claret, optic. $150.00.
4) Violet Mt. Vernon #1 nine ounce goblet. $200.00.
5) Violet Everglade #2 candlestick. $300.00.
6) Violet Jenny Lind #321, 8" dish, crimped. $350.00.

Row 4

1) Ivory #198 perfume. $150.00.
2) Ivory Wetherford 8" nappy. $125.00.
3) Ivory #25 eight ounce syrup and cover, black enamel trim. $250.00.
4) Windsor Blue Daisy and Button hat made for John Degenhart. $100.00.
5) Windsor Blue Seashell #SS44, 6" flower center. $225.00.
6) Windsor Blue Statuesque #3011, 9" candle stick. $600.00.

Plate 51

Topaz is included on this comparison page to demonstrate that it belongs in the yellow family of colors which is readily apparent when viewed side by side with various shades of green glass. On the extreme left side of Row 2 is a Stradivari or Regency cocktail in an unusual shade of green. Only a few pieces in this green shade are known. Forest Green and Late Dark Emerald are difficult to identify based on color alone. However, there was little, if any, duplication of pieces made in these two colors; thus, once the collector becomes familiar with the blanks and their time periods, the color becomes readily identified. Early Emerald was strictly a Nearcut era color and again the pieces indicate the color.

Row 1

1) Topaz #54, 7" footed bowl or comport. $75.00.
2) Topaz Georgian #319 nine ounce tumbler. $75.00.
3) Topaz Stratford #5 two-pint jug, signed. $250.00.
4) Early Dark Emerald Thistle #2766 tumbler, gold encrusted, signed "NEARCUT." $35.00.
5) Early Dark Emerald Thistle #2766 spooner, gold encrusted, signed "NEARCUT." $60.00.

Row 2

1) "Odd Green" Stradivari #3575, 3½ ounce cocktail. $60.00.
2) Pistachio Martha #250 individual creamer. $20.00.
3) Pistachio Georgian #319/B/2 basket, Crystal handle. $60.00.
4) Pistachio Martha #250 individual sugar. $20.00.
5) Light Emerald Georgian #317S sherbet. $20.00.
6) Light Emerald #968 two-piece cocktail icer, Decagon insert. $45.00.
7) Light Emerald #3400/79 tall six ounce oil, Crystal foot. $125.00.

Row 3

1) Light Emerald #3400 seven ounce lunch goblet, etched Apple Blossom. $50.00.
2) Light Emerald #3130 three ounce cocktail, etched Apple Blossom, gold encrusted. $45.00.
3) Light Emerald Decagon #638, 6" three-lite candlestick. $40.00.
4) Light Emerald #299, 5" candy box and cover, three-footed. $50.00.
5) Light Emerald #510 temple jar, Ebony lid. $175.00.

Row 4

1) Forest Green #611, 8 ounce stein. $40.00.
2) Forest Green Tally-Ho #1402/96 twin salad dressing bowl. $60.00.
3) Forest Green Nautilus #3450, 10 ounce tumbler. $20.00.
4) Late Dark Emerald Caprice #151, 5" two-handled jelly. $35.00.
5) Late Dark Emerald #496, 12 ounce Tall Joe tumbler. $20.00.
6) Late Dark Emerald #1066 seven ounce tall sherbet, Crystal stem and foot. $15.00.

Plate 52

Moonlight is a slightly darker blue than Willow Blue. Color identification, in most instances, can be made by the piece. Moonlight was used primarily for Caprice and the Gyro Optic lines while Willow Blue dates to the late 1920s and the early to middle 1930s and was used for the lines and blanks prevalent during those years. There was some production of Moonlight Everglade line pieces during the late 1930s and early 1940s.

Blue Bell is a distinct color and will not be confused with the other Cambridge blues.

Blue 1 is darker than Willow Blue and Moonlight but somewhat lighter than Ritz Blue.

The Royal Blues are the darkest of all the blues and the early version can be distinguished by the piece.

Ritz Blue, darker than Blue 1, was primarily used in conjunction with the Decagon line and can be identified in that manner.

Row 1
1) Willow Blue Moderne #3300 five ounce low sherbet. $15.00.
2) Willow Blue #3120 six ounce tall sherbet, etched #733. $30.00.
3) Willow Blue #3077 eight ounce fruit salad. $25.00.
4) Moonlight Caprice #100 five ounce oil, no stopper. $100.00.
5) Moonlight Jefferson #1401, 12 ounce iced tea. $20.00.
6) Moonlight Caprice #235, 6" four-footed rose bowl, with 4" flower block. $250.00.

Row 2
1) Blue Bell #3075 six ounce low sherbet, etched #731. $45.00.
2) Blue Bell eight ounce dog bottle. $125.00.
3) Blue Bell Wetherford 4" nappy. $50.00.
4) Blue I #124, 3½" basket. $75.00.
5) Blue I #447 two-piece mayonnaise set, unidentified floral cutting. $65.00.

Row 3
1) Royal Blue #3400/68 sugar, signed. $30.00.
2) Royal Blue Mt. Vernon #1 nine ounce goblet. $40.00.
3) Royal Blue #3400/68 creamer, signed. $30.00.
4) Ritz Blue Mt. Vernon #2, 6½ ounce tall sherbet. $35.00.
5) Ritz Blue Decagon #865 cup and saucer, signed. $25.00.

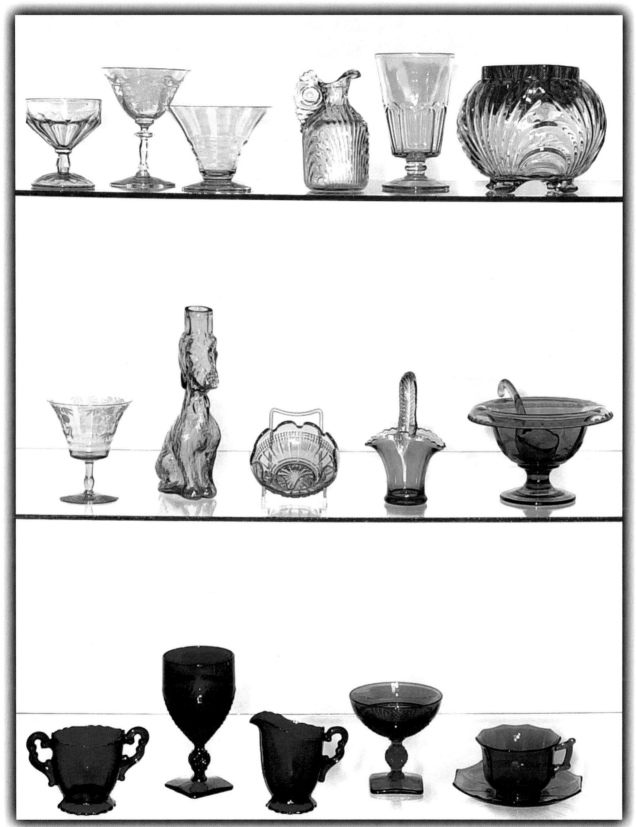

Plate 53

Mulberry from the 1920s and the Late Mulberry are lighter shades than Amethyst. As is true for a number of colors, the piece gives a clue as to the color. As far as it is known, Mulberry and Amethyst were never used for the same piece as Mulberry had been discontinued by the time Amethyst was introduced.

Late Pink presents a problem in that it is so close to Peach-blo that it can only be definitively identified when the piece is unique to the color's production period, 1955 – 1959. However the problem is not of great magnitude since so little was made and very few shapes were duplicated in both colors.

La Rosa was used primarily in conjunction with the Caprice and Gyro Optic lines while Peach-blo was not. All etched pink pieces are Peach-blo.

The Crown Tuscan pieces seen here are arranged with the darker pieces on the left, shifting to the lighter pieces on the right. There is considerable variation in the color but there is no evidence to suggest there is a distinct second color.

Row 1
1) Mulberry #3077 nine ounce goblet. $40.00.
2) Mulberry #2206 three-piece mayonnaise set. $60.00.
3) Mulberry #2810 puff box and cover. $75.00.
4) Amethyst #1337 cigarette holder, Crystal stem and foot, unidentified cutting. $75.00.
5) Amethyst #497 ranch tumbler, spiral optic. $20.00.
6) Amethyst #1066, 11 ounce goblet, Crystal stem and foot. $25.00.

Row 2
1) Heatherbloom Martha Washington #1400, 10 ounce goblet. $85.00.
2) Heatherbloom Martha Washington #56, 12 ounce stein. $85.00.
3) Heatherbloom #3400/68 sugar, signed, etched Gloria. $50.00.
4) Heatherbloom #3035 six ounce tall sherbet, Crystal stem and foot, etched #731. $75.00.
5) Late Mulberry Caprice #301 sherbet, pale gold stem and foot. $150.00.
6) Late Mulberry #3400/92, 32 ounce ball decanter. $40.00.

Row 3
1) Pink #1529 decanter, no stopper. $75.00.
2) Pink Invitation #3791, 12 ounce footed tumbler. $25.00.
3) La Rosa Caprice #235, 6" four-footed rose bowl. $250.00.
4) Peach-blo #642 ashtray. $45.00.
5) Peach-blo Moderne #3300 five ounce high sherbet. $20.00.
6) Peach-blo #3115, 10 ounce footed tumbler, Crystal stem and foot, etched Valencia. $50.00.

Row 4
1) Crown Tuscan #1337 cigarette holder, ebony ashtray foot. $350.00.
2) Crown Tuscan #3400/45, 11" four-toed bowl, fancy edge, Crown Tuscan signature, etched Portia, gold encrusted, exterior gold trim. $250.00.
3) Crown Tuscan #3500/1 cup and saucer. $125.00.
4) Crown Tuscan #511 "Tombstone" bookend. $300.00.

Plate 54

Mocha was used almost exclusively in conjunction with the Caprice and Gyro Optic lines while the somewhat similar Madeira dates to 1929 – 1930 and was used with blanks and shapes from that era. Etched pieces are always Madeira.

Both the 1920s Amber and the Amber that replaced Madeira are darker than Madeira or Mocha and should not be confused with either of those two colors. Distinguishing between these twos ambers is on the basis of the blank or piece when possible at all. Some variation in color is noticed, probably due to minor formula changes, but the color name remained Amber. The reorganized company significantly changed the formula and produced a much darker shade but retained the name Amber. Today, it is recommended this color be called Late Dark Amber and it is readily distinguishable from the earlier Amber.

Mandarin Gold is noticeably darker than Gold Krystol. As is true for many colors, knowledge of the time frame in which a piece was produced is a good clue as to the color's identity. Topaz is not confused with either Mandarin Gold or Gold Krystol since it is an entirely different shade of yellow.

Row 1

1) Mocha #1066 seven ounce tall sherbet, Crystal stem and foot. $15.00.
2) Mocha Caprice #38 sugar, medium size. $30.00.
3) Mocha Caprice #38 creamer, medium size. $30.00.
4) Madeira 3400/55 cream soup, signed, etched Brettone. $30.00.
5) Madeira Tally-Ho #1402/8 five ounce low stem juice. $15.00.

Row 2

1) Amber #620 three-piece sugar, creamer and tray set, signed. $35.00.
2) Amber #617 cigarette jar and cover, etched #731. $75.00.
3) Amber #3400/102, 5" globe vase. $40.00.
4) Amber Wild Rose #3200 five ounce punch cup. $40.00.
5) Amber #3400, 22 ounce jug on Farber chrome base. $45.00.

Row 3

1) Gold Krystol #3400/38, 12 ounce tumbler, etched Apple Blossom. $40.00.
2) Gold Krystol #1312, 3½" cigarette box and cover, Crystal stem and foot. $85.00.
3) Gold Krystol Decagon #867 creamer, etched Lorna. $25.00.
4) Mandarin Gold #1066 seven ounce tall sherbet. $15.00.
5) Mandarin Gold Georgian #319, 12 ounce tumbler. $20.00.
6) Mandarin Gold Pristine #P499 calla lily candlestick. $40.00.

Row 4

1) Late Amber Jenny Lind #318, 8¼" basket, no handle. $60.00.
2) Late Amber Jenny Lind mayonnaise bowl. $35.00.
3) Topaz #680 dresser compact. $100.00.
4) Topaz #7801 five ounce roemer, Crystal stem and foot. $50.00.

Plate 55

115

Beginning with its first catalog and continuing until the second company closed its doors, Cambridge produced blown and pressed stemware. Early production was in crystal or colorless glass but by the 1920s color was playing an important role in the many Cambridge stemware lines. Stemware in color continued to be offered right up until the end of the second company. This plate illustrates some of the lines produced with a colored bowl, stem, or foot and combinations thereof.

Row 1

1) Pistachio Gyro Optic #3143, 10 ounce goblet, Crystal stem and foot. $65.00.
2) Amber Mt. Vernon #1 nine ounce goblet. $25.00.
3) Forest Green Tally-Ho #1402/2, 14 ounce goblet. $25.00.
4) Amethyst Tally-Ho 1402/100 low sherbet, Crystal stem and foot. $35.00.
5) Blue Bell #3075 one ounce cordial, optic. $125.00.
6) Peach-blo #7606, 10 ounce goblet, narrow optic. $25.00.
7) Crystal #3103 nine ounce goblet, Forest Green stem, Crystal foot. $35.00.
8) Carmen #3104, 3½ ounce cocktail, Crystal stem and foot. $150.00.

Row 2

1) Amber #3500, 10 ounce goblet, long bowl, Crystal stem and foot. $30.00.
2) Royal Blue #3105 Pressed Rose Point sherbet, Crystal stem and foot. $75.00.
3) Heatherbloom #3035, 12 ounce footed tumbler, Crystal stem and foot, etched #731. $85.00.
4) Heatherbloom #1066, 11 ounce goblet, Crystal stem and foot, etched Gloria. $125.00.
5) Gold Krystol Deauville #3125 goblet, Crystal stem and foot, etched Deauville. $60.00.
6) Royal Blue #3126 three ounce cocktail, Crystal stem and foot. $45.00.
7) Avocado #3085, 4½ ounce claret, optic. $150.00.
8) Amber #3122 nine ounce footed tumbler, Crystal stem and foot, etched Portia. $50.00.

Row 3

1) Carmen Cambridge Square #3798, 12 ounce iced tea, Crystal stem and foot. $125.00
2) Azurite #21, 3½ ounce sherbet. $75.00.
3) Crystal #3140 cocktail, Light Emerald stem and foot. $35.00.
4) Crown Tuscan #7966 two ounce sherry. $150.00.
5) Amethyst #3035, 12 ounce footed tumbler, Crystal stem and foot. $30.00.
6) Moonlight Caprice #2 seven ounce tall sherbet. $30.00.
7) Peach-blo #3015 nine ounce goblet, etched #742. $40.00.
8) Forest Green Martha Washington #1400, 10 ounce goblet. $30.00.

Row 4

1) Amethyst #3078, 6½ ounce tall sherbet. $20.00.
2) Light Emerald #3135 eight ounce goblet, etched Apple Blossom. $50.00.
3) Mandarin Gold Today #A56 goblet. $25.00.
4) Moonlight Jefferson #1401 five ounce footed tumbler before foot is finished. $75.00.
5) Gold Krystol #3025, 10 ounce goblet, Amber stem and foot, etched Gloria. $85.00.
6) Light Emerald #1069, 11 ounce goblet, Crystal foot. $50.00.
7) Amber #3051 nine ounce goblet, narrow optic. $20.00.
8) Moonlight Caprice #300 five ounce parfait. $175.00.

Plate 56

117

Also known as the 3011 line, Lady Figure Line and "The Cambridge Nudes," this line, or at least parts of it, was produced from 1931 until the second company ceased operations. Very popular with today's collectors, the abundant amount available indicates the line's popularity during the years it was produced. While the regular cocktail (3011/9) was made in the most colors, all items came in a range of colors. Unless otherwise specified, all of the "nude stems" shown here are Crystal and not frosted.

Row 1
1) Crown Tuscan #3011, 9" candlestick. $150.00.
2) Topaz #3011/11 three ounce "tulip" cocktail. $750.00.
3) Royal Blue #3011/1 banquet goblet. $400.00.
4) Carmen #3011/40, 10" flower or fruit center aka "Flying Lady Bowl." $4,000.00.
5) Royal Blue #3011, cigarette holder. $850.00.
6) Carmen #3011/28 covered candy box, satin stem. $2,000.00.

Row 2
1) Mandarin Gold #SS11, 7" comport. $450.00.
2) Royal Blue #3011/14 one ounce cordial. $450.00.
3) Forest Green #3011/10 three ounce "V shaped" cocktail. $650.00.
4) Carmen #3011/25 ivy ball. $300.00.
5) Pistachio #3011 three ounce cocktail, middle size Nude stem. $275.00.
6) Crown Tuscan #3011, 7" comport, flared, gold trim. $250.00.
7) Royal Blue #3011/12 three ounce wine. $325.00.
8) Windsor Blue #3011, 9" candlestick, Crystal bobeche and prisms. $900.00.

Row 3
1) Royal Blue #3011/26 bud vase. $750.00.
2) Gold Krystol #3011 cigarette box and cover, largest Nude stem. $450.00.
3) Amethyst #3011/9 three ounce cocktail. $100.00.
4) Royal Blue #3011 covered sweetmeat. $2,000.00.
5) Amber #3011/27, 5⅜" wide blown comport. $350.00.
6) Royal Blue #3011/8, 4½ ounce sauterne. $400.00.
7) Pink Crackle #3011/3 saucer champagne. $650.00.

Row 4
1) Smoke #3011/2 table goblet. $300.00.
2) Pistachio #3011 ashtray. $350.00.
3) Forest Green #3011/7, 4½ ounce claret. $125.00.
4) Carmen 7" cupped comport, middle size Nude stem. $275.00.
5) Royal Blue #3011/5 six ounce hoch. $600.00.
6) Crown Tuscan #3011 cigarette box and cover, middle size Nude stem, black enamel trim. $1,250.00.

Plate 57

Cambridge was noted for its line of figural flower holders, pieces based on similar items produced and sold in Europe. Also known as flower frogs, these began appearing in the Cambridge catalog during the 1920s and, in Crystal, a few were still listed on the October 1956 price list. The latter included the 9" Heron, Sea Gull, 8½" "Draped Lady," and the 6" "Bashful Charlotte." When the 1958 and final price list was issued, none of the figural flower holders were offered. The names "Draped Lady," "Bashful Charlotte," "Mandolin Lady," "Giesha," and "Bird on Stump" were adopted by collectors and are not original to Cambridge.

Row 1
1) Topaz 9½" Oriental figure with two hair buns. $450.00.
2) Ivory "Draped Lady" figure. $350.00.
3) Jade 10" "Geisha" figure with one hair bun.*
4) Ivory #512, 9½" Rose Lady figure flower holder, enamel and gold trim. $1,250.00.
5) Blue Bell #513, 13½" "Draped Lady" figure flower holder. $1,800.00.
6) Crystal #1115, 11" "Bashful Charlotte" figure flower holder. $150.00.

Row 2
1) Pink (very pale) #509, 8¾" Two Kid figure flower holder. $250.00.
2) Ivory #509, 8¾" Two Kid figure flower holder. $2,000.00.
3) Amber #509, 8¾" Two Kid figure flower holder. $300.00.
4) Light Emerald "Bird on Stump" figure flower holder, satin finish. $275.00.
5) Peach-blo #512, 9½" Rose Lady figure flower holder, satin finish. $225.00.
6) Light Emerald #512, 9½" Rose Lady figure flower holder, satin finish. $225.00.

Row 3
1) Moonlight #518, 8½" "Draped Lady" figure flower holder. $300.00.
2) Amber #518, 8½" "Draped Lady" figure flower holder, satin finish. $200.00.
3) Light Emerald #518, 8½" "Draped Lady" figure flower holder. $150.00.
4) Gold Krystol #518, 8½" "Draped Lady" figure flower holder. $200.00.
5) Light Emerald #1108, 9¼" "Mandolin Lady" figure flower holder. $250.00.
6) Crystal #1136, 9" Heron figure flower holder. $85.00.

Row 4
1) Ebony #2899, 5" flower block, marked "PAT'D APR 11, 1916." $45.00.
2) Peach-blo #2899, 3½" flower block, marked "PAT'D APR 11, 1916." $25.00.
3) Peach-blo #703 flower holder with #2899, 3" flower block. $45.00.
4) Crown Tuscan #70 Turtle flower holder. $800.00.
5) Madeira #2899, 5" flower holder, marked "PAT'D APR 11, 1916." $45.00.
6) Azurite #2899, 2½" flower block. $75.00.
7) Ebony #70 Turtle flower holder. $350.00.
8) Crystal #1138, 8½" Sea Gull figure flower holder. $50.00.

Plate 58

Another important aspect of the Cambridge line was its production of swans in sizes ranging from 3" to the 16" punch bowl. Very popular with collectors, the swans come in a wide range of colors and feather detail. The major classification of the latter being Style I, Style II, and Style III, a discussion of which is is beyond the scope of this book.

Row 1
1) Mocha, #1040, 3" Style II, signed. $75.00.
2) Ebony, #1040, 3" Style II, signed. $60.00.
3) Crystal, satin finished #1040, 3" Style II, signed, enameled beak and fins. $200.00.
4) Moonlight #1043, 8½" Style III, signed, with rose knob lid. $4,000.00.
5) Light Emerald #1040, 3" Style II, signed, gold trim. $75.00.
6) Amber #1040, 3" Style II, signed. $75.00.
7) Forest Green #1040, 3" Style II. $100.00.

Row 2
1) Gold Krystol #1043, 8½" Style I, signed. $250.00.
2) Light Emerald #1045, 12½" Style I, signed. $500.00.
3) Heather Pink* #1040, 3" Style I, signed. $85.00.
4) Ebony #1044, 10½" Style I, signed. $350.00.

Row 3
1) Carmen #1042, 6½" Style III. $250.00.
2) Milk Glass #1043, 8½" Style III. $300.00.
3) Milk Glass #1040, 3" Style III, gold trim. $85.00.
4) Peach-blo #1042, 6½" Style I, signed. $100.00.
5) Light Emerald #1041, 4½" Style I, signed. $60.00.

Row 4
1) Late Dark Emerald #1043, 8½" Style III. $125.00.
2) Mandarin Gold #1042, 6½" Style III. $100.00.
3) Crystal #1041, 4½" Style III. $25.00.
4) Crown Tuscan #1043, 8½" Style III, gold trim. $175.00.

*Color named by collectors.

Plate 59

Many collectors are limited to what they can collect because of the available space to hold the collection. These people turn to cordials, salt and pepper shakers, salt dips, and other items of a similar size. Then there are those at the other end of the spectrum who, while they may not have unlimited space, do have enough to collect and display the larger items produced by Cambridge.

From the early years on until the second company ceased operations, punch bowls were in the Cambridge line. From the Nearcut era there are punch bowls in the Marjorie, Feather, Dorothy, Colonial, and Ribbon lines plus others. These were followed by others, each successive line based on the current trends in glass design. Around 1915 – 1916, Cambridge introduced several lines that had the basic pattern pressed but then was enhanced by cutting.

One such line was No. 3200 Cut Wild Rose Design and among pieces in the line was a punch bowl. The rose on the bowl, pedestal base, and cup would have been enhanced by cutting. Later, the added cutting was discontinued and then the proper name became Wild Rose or just 3200. Produced in Crystal during the early years, this punch bowl remained in the Cambridge line until the demise of the second company. Seen here in Carmen, it is also known in Amber and in Crystal.

The Tally-Ho line, also known as the #1402 line, was introduced in 1932. Included in it was the 1402/77 13" footed punch bowl. Completing the punch set was a 17" tray and a six-ounce punch mug. Also available was a footed punch cup, much like the coffee cup in appearance. Produced until the mid-1940s, the Tally-Ho punch bowl was made in Carmen, Royal Blue, Amber, Crystal, and Forest Green.

Created as a display fixture, primarily for millinery stores, the mannequin head never appeared in Cambridge general line catalogs. Dating to the 1930s, it is rarely seen today, and is in few collections. This writer recalls seeing one in a New England beauty shop window many years ago. The owner had no idea of its origins other than it had been a gift from a friend and would not part with it for sentimental reasons. The mannequin head is known in Crown Tuscan, Amber, Peach-blo, Crystal, and Ebony.

Top Left
Amber Mannequin Head. $4,000.00.

Top Right
Royal Blue Tally-Ho #1402/77, 13" footed punch bowl; 12 x 1402/78 six ounce punch mugs; 1402/29, 17" tray. $850.00.

Bottom
Carmen Wild Rose #3200 punch bowl and base. $1,500.00.

Plate 60

The National Cambridge Collectors, Inc., opened its first museum in June 1982. It was located on Route 40 just east of the Cambridge city limits. It served the organization well, albeit with limited space, until June 1998 when devastating floods hit the area. While little of the collection was lost, the building itself suffered major damage and the organization decided not to rebuild on the same site. A suitable existing building was found in downtown Cambridge that, other than the construction of some 60 display cases, required no major remodeling. The new facility opened its doors on April 1, 2002, and shortly thereafter, officially became known as The National Museum of Cambridge Glass. In addition to the main display area, the museum has a research library, an educational room, a small auditorium, a gift shop, and special display areas. The glass illustrated on previous pages is but a small portion of the collection to be seen in the main display area.

The special display areas consist of three rooms and the glass in these rooms is changed each year. The first area consists of display cases and each year they are filled with glass from one or more private collections. The second room houses a re-creation of the Cambridge factory sample room while the third is a re-creation of a dining room as it might have appeared in the home of Mr. and Mrs. Arthur J. Bennett. It is these latter two rooms that are seen on the opposing page.

Currently, the dining room is as it might have looked on Christmas day. The table is set with Carmen place settings, some items being etched and gold encrusted. On the buffet sits a Carmen Wild Rose punch bowl filled with Christmas ornaments. On the wall hang photographic portraits of Mr. and Mrs. Bennett. Unfortunately, none of the fixtures, furniture, place settings, or other glassware are original to the Bennett home.

The second room shown is the re-creation of a portion of the factory sample rooms. The display units are original and have been restored to their original appearance with much paint having been removed. The picture on the left is of Mr. Wilbur L. Orme, Sr., son-in-law of Mr. Bennett and company president following Mr. Bennett's 1940 death. On the right is a photographic portrait of Mary Martha Mitchell, who began her career at Cambridge as a stenographer/clerk and later became secretary to Mr. Bennett and then to Mr. Orme. She rose up through the ranks of the reorganized company's management to become the last president of the Cambridge Glass Co. Hanging on the wall between the two display units is a clock that once hung in the office of the company treasurer.

Plate 61

Mission Statement

The National Cambridge Collectors, Inc., is a non-profit Ohio corporation founded in 1973 to establish and maintain a permanent museum in Cambridge, Ohio, for the display, study, and preservation of Cambridge glass. Part of the mission includes accumulating and publishing information related to the Cambridge Glass Co.

About NCC, Inc.

Membership — Membership in the National Cambridge Collectors, Inc. is available to all interested individuals. Please check our website at www.Cambridgeglass.org for the latest information regarding membership.

Newsletter — One of the benefits of membership in the National Cambridge Collectors is the newsletter known as the *Cambridge Crystal Ball*. This publication informs members of happenings within the club and in most issues there is a detailed article relating to some phase of Cambridge glass, such as a study of a particular pattern or historical information about the company.

Cambridge Study Groups — These are groups of members who live fairly close to one another and who hold regular meetings where they study topics related to Cambridge glass. Study groups are often involved in projects, including ones related to fund-raising, that benefit the museum as well as the organization as a whole.

Publications — In addition to this volume, NCC, Inc., offers a range of publications including catalog reprints, books on etchings and cuttings, small books on individual etchings, and numerous other books.

The National Museum of Cambridge Glass — The crowning achievement of NCC, Inc., has been the creation of The National Museum of Cambridge Glass, located in downtown Cambridge, Ohio. The museum is open April 1 to October 31, Wednesday through Sunday, except that it is closed Easter Sunday and July 4.

Annual Convention — Every summer, toward the end of June, NCC, Inc., holds a convention in Cambridge, Ohio. The convention is a place where members gather to have fun, attend the organization's annual meeting, listen to seminars by guest speakers, and attend a glass show featuring some of the best Cambridge glass dealers in the country. In addition to the glass show, there is a "mini-show," usually on Saturday morning, that features additional dealers selling Cambridge glass.

Additional Information — For additional information on any of the above topics, as well as more information about National Cambridge Collectors, Inc., and its activities, interested readers are urged to contact NCC, Inc., via its website at www.Cambridgeglass.org, by postal mail at PO Box 416, Cambridge, OH 43725-0416, or by telephone during the museum season at (740) 432-4245.